A Garland Series

OUTSTANDING DISSERTATIONS IN THE

FINE ARTS

Francis William Edmonds

Mammon and Art

Maybelle Mann

Garland Publishing, Inc., New York & London

1977

Library of Congress Cataloging in Publication Data

Mann, Maybelle.
  Francis William Edmonds, Mammon and art.

  (Outstanding dissertations in the fine arts)
  Originally presented as the author's thesis,
New York University, 1972.
  Bibliography: p.
  1. Edmonds, Francis William, 1806-1863.
2. Painters--United States--Biography. I. Title.
II. Series.
ND237.E394M36 1977   759.13 [B]   76-23638
ISBN 0-8240-2708-6

Printed in the United States of America

INTRODUCTION

From the time this dissertation was written much new information, paintings and sketches have emerged. Some of it sheds additional light on Edmonds' life and activities and some has served to strengthen original hypotheses.

Artistically, specific evidence has been found to support a claim that Edmonds influenced genre painting in subject matter and composition. The Penny Paper, exhibited in 1839, before Edmonds traveled abroad, is one of the earliest to introduce the ragged newsboy as a theme. His influence on contemporaries is noticeable in the work of Tompkins Matteson and Eastman Johnson selected a number of the same titles.

Oil sketches have surfaced that support Edmonds' statement that he painted from life. The portrait of Baby Mary attests to the accuracy of his vision, because several of his direct descendants bear striking resemblances to this picture.

The questions that were raised about Edmonds' devotion to his children have been partially answered with the location of warm and devoted letters from the children to their father.

Edmonds' importance in the cultural art world of New York City has been confirmed by the discovery of his involvement in the creation of the Crystal Palace for New York and by more detailed accounts of his activities in the New-York Gallery of Fine Arts.

The International Exhibition Foundation funded the national show of Edmonds' works (1975-76) that was accompanied by my catalogue. Additional funds came from the National Endowment for the Arts. Articles on various aspects of Edmonds' life and work have appeared in magazines and more are forthcoming.

FRANCIS WILLIAM EDMONDS: MAMMON AND ART

A dissertation in the Department of American Civilization
submitted to the faculty of the Graduate School of Arts
and Science in partial fulfillment of the requirements for
the degree of Doctor of Philosophy at New York University.

Maybelle Mann

Adviser: Robert J. Goldwater

Granted (Month)_____(Year)_____

TABLE OF CONTENTS

PREFACE

The purpose of this study is to place Francis William
Edmonds, 1806-1863, in his proper perspective in the art,
cultural and business worlds that were part of his life.
Generally regarded as a part-time artist and bank cashier,
Edmonds made contributions to all these fields that were
substantial and out of the ordinary. Primary documents,
consisting of autobiographical manuscripts and diaries,
serve to cast new light on some old ideas of antebellum
activities in these diverse fields.

The internal affairs of the American Art-Union, the
National Academy of Design and the New-York Gallery of Fine
Arts come under scrutiny in the examination of the major
role played by Edmonds in these organizations. Edmonds'
position as the only Academician from the National Academy
on the board of managers of the American Art-Union was a
unique situation.

As an artist, Edmonds was deeply concerned with the
art of other men of the past and of his contemporaries. He
wrote extensive opinions of the art he viewed in Europe during a sojourn of eight months in 1841, which in comparison
with contemporary opinions demonstrate the originality of
Edmonds' thought.

Through notations in Edmonds' journal, I believe I
have identified art instructional material that contributed to the esthetic ideals of American artists. This
conflicts with other suggestions that they exhibited a
striking lack of esthetic doctrine and ideas, unlike the
neo-classicists and romanticists of Europe who fought over
the issues. It is true that there was no conflict among
the artists in America, but it is not true that they
brought no esthetic ideals into the exercise of their art.
The impact of nationalism and other contributing factors
to this esthetic are discussed and evaluated.

Extensive research into the newspapers and magazines
of the day produced many contemporary reviews, descriptions and titles of pictures by Edmonds, not known before.
The reviews are important for what they reveal of the
mores and of the attitudes towards art and life in antebellum America.

The complex life Edmonds led exhibits how closely the
worlds of art, culture and business could be intertwined.
Edmonds was extolled for compartmentalizing his activities,
but in actuality they were one. His engraving and art interests were inextricably enmeshed with his business and
banking, while his banking position was an asset in finding
backers for the New-York Gallery of Fine Arts.

Prior to this thesis, the only published material on
Edmonds has been in the standard reference works. An

article by Sybil Brush in The Villager of Bronxville, N.Y. in March 1966 dealt mainly with the house Edmonds built there. The author wrote a short article on Edmonds that appeared in the American Art Journal in the Fall '70 issue.

Dr. Irwin Unger suggested the book on 19th century banking by Fritz Redlich. Through information in Redlich's book, a self-portrait (Figure 1) of Edmonds was found at the New York Clearing House. The personnel at the Clearing House, who were kind enough to show the portrait, advised where the donor of the portrait, Mr. Francis Edmonds Tyng, could be located.

This study was made more viable through the autobiographical manuscripts that were made available to me by Mr. and Mrs. Francis Edmonds Tyng. Through their continued cooperation, the diary of 1854 was discovered in the possession of Mrs. Dorothy Coffeen. The diary is not signed, but I was able to match the events and people mentioned in the diary with those known to have been in Edmonds' life.

The travel journal was discovered by tracing all the immediate Edmonds' descendants. Murray Johnson, the attorney for the last survivor of the Edmonds' children, donated all the Edmonds' artifacts to the Columbia County Historical Society in Kinderhook, N.Y. Mrs. Allen J. Thomas, Jr. of the Columbia County Historical Society gave invaluable assistance, not only in duplicating documents,

but in tracing other records. Mrs. Eugene Moskowitz, historian of St. Paul's Church, Eastchester, N.Y., investi-
gated records and provided the photograph of Felix Trembled
hanging in St. Paul's.

Canon Edward N. West of the Cathedral Church of St.
John the Divine suggested the connection between the painting Felix Trembled and the story of Bishop Benjamin Tredwell Onderdonk. Mr. William Crapo, Coordinator of Diocesan
Missions of the Episcopal Diocese of New York was invaluable in unearthing the picture. Mrs. David Bartlett,
Village Historian for Bronxville, N.Y., introduced me to
Dr. and Mrs. Dicran Goulian, the present owners of the
home Edmonds built in Bronxville.

It was Dr. Barbara Novak who first suggested Francis
William Edmonds as a subject for investigation and later
suggested that it would be suitable for a dissertation.
Evelyn Samuels at Fine Arts Institute was helpful with
library information. Last, but not least, Dr. Robert J.
Goldwater provided the guidance and criticisms for this
thesis.

LIST OF ILLUSTRATIONS

List of abbreviations:

NAD---National Academy of Design

Cat.--Catalogue

AAU---American Art-Union

Figure 1. Francis William Edmonds: Self-portrait, oil on canvas, New York Clearing House, donated by Francis Edmonds Tyng.
(photo: courtesy of the American Art Journal).

Figure 2. Francis William Edmonds: The Epicure, oil on canvas. Descendant in California. NAD Cat. No. 286 under E.F. Williams, 1838.
(photo: courtesy descendant).

Figure 3. Francis William Edmonds: Commodore Trunnion and Jack Hatchway, oil on canvas. Private collection. NAD Cat. No. 251, 1839.
(photo: courtesy private collector).

Figure 4. Francis William Edmonds: Sparking, oil on canvas. Sterling and Francine Clark Art Institute, Inventory No. 916 (P). NAD Cat. No. 234, 1840.
(photo: courtesy of the Sterling and Francine Clark Art Institute).

Figure 5. Francis William Edmonds: The City and Country Beaux, oil on canvas. Sterling and Francine Clark Art Institute, Accession No. 50.915. NAD Cat. No. 230, 1840.
(photo: courtesy of the Sterling and Francine Clark Art Institute).

Figure 6. Asher B. Durand: Portrait of Francis William Edmonds, oil on canvas. National Academy of Design.
(photo: courtesy the National Academy of Design).

Figure 7. Francis William Edmonds: The Image Peddler, oil on canvas. New-York Historical Society, Accession No. 1858.71. NAD Cat. No. 205, 1844.
(photo: courtesy New-York Historical Society).

Figure 8. Francis William Edmonds: Head of a man, oil on convas. Private collection. (photo: courtesy private collector).

Figure 9. Francis William Edmonds: Pencil and wash sketch of man and dog, untitled. Prints Division, New York Public Library, Accession No. 84953. (photo: courtesy New York Public Library).

Figure 10. Francis William Edmonds: Pencil and wash sketch of boat, untitled. Prints Division, New York Public Library, Accession No. 84952. (photo: courtesy New York Public Library).

Figure 11. Francis William Edmonds: Facing the Enemy, oil sketch on board. Private collection. Original NAD Cat. No. 114, 1845. (photo: courtesy private collector).

Figure 12. William Sidney Mount: Loss and Gain, oil on canvas. Collection of Mr. and Mrs. J. William Middendorf, II. AAU Cat. No. 246, 1848. (photo: courtesy of Mr. and Mrs. J. William Middendorf, II).

Figure 13. Francis William Edmonds: The Organ-Grinder, oil on canvas. Exhibited at the American Art-Union as The Strolling Musician, Cat. No. 2, 1848. Collection of Mr. and Mrs. John Heinz, III. (photo: courtesy of Mr. and Mrs. John Heinz, III).

Figure 14. Francis William Edmonds: The Schoolmaster, oil on canvas. Exhibited as The Two Culprits, NAD Cat. No. 211, 1850. Location unknown. (photo: courtesy Kennedy Galleries).

Figure 15. Francis William Edmonds: Crow's Nest, gouache on brown paper, November 1851. Private collection. (photo: courtesy private collector).

Figure 16. Francis William Edmonds: The Real Estate Agent, oil on canvas. D.D. Eisenhower Collection, but reported lost. Exhibited as The Speculator, NAD Cat. No. 230, 1852. (photo: Montclair Art Museum Bulletin, March, 1947).

Figure 17. Francis William Edmonds: The Paper City, wash drawing, 1838. New-York Historical Society, Accession No. 1944.386. (photo: courtesy of The New-York Historical Society).

Figure 18. Francis William Edmonds: <u>Taking the Census</u>, oil on canvas. Private collection. NAD Cat. No. 162, 1854.
(photo: private collector).

Figure 19. Francis William Edmonds: <u>Felix Trembled</u>, oil on canvas. Seen as originally hung in St. Paul's Episcopal Church, Eastchester, N.Y., December 1855.
(photo: courtesy Mrs. Eugene Moskowitz, Church Historian).

Figure 20: Francis William Edmonds: <u>The Scythe Grinder</u>, oil on canvas. New-York Historical Society, Accession No. 1947.493, 1856.
(photo: courtesy The New-York Historical Society).

Figure 21. William Sidney Mount: <u>Who'll Turn the Grindstone</u>, oil on canvas. The Suffolk Museum at Stony Brook, Long Island, Accession No. 0. 1. 18.
(photo: courtesy of the Suffolk Museum at Stony Brook, L.I.).

Figure 22. Francis William Edmonds: <u>All Talk and No Work</u>, oil on canvas. The Brooklyn Museum, Accession No. 51.108. NAD Cat. No. 61, 1856.
(photo: courtesy of The Brooklyn Museum).

Figure 23. Francis William Edmonds: <u>The Pan of Milk</u>, oil on canvas. The New-York Historical Society, R.L. Stuart Collection, No. 49. NAD Cat. No. 537, 1858.
(photo: courtesy The New-York Historical Society).

Figure 24. Francis William Edmonds: <u>The Christmas Turkey</u>, oil on canvas. The New-York Historical Society, R.L. Stuart Collection, No. 50. Exhibited at the NAD as <u>Bargaining</u>, Cat. No. 616, 1858.
(photo: courtesy of The New-York Historical Society).

Figure 25. Francis William Edmonds: <u>The Wind-Mill</u>, oil on canvas. The New-York Historical Society, R.L. Stuart Collection, No. 51. NAD Cat. No. 232, 1858.
(photo: courtesy The New-York Historical Society).

Figure 26. Francis William Edmonds: <u>Reading the Scriptures</u>, oil on canvas. Exhibited 1858 at an "Artists Reception," New York. Private collection.
(photo: courtesy private collector).

Figure 27. Francis William Edmonds: <u>Hard Times</u>, oil on canvas. Location unknown. Listed in the Cat. of the Chronological Exhibition of the Brooklyn Art Association, April 1872, as exhibited at the Artists' Fund Society 1861, under title <u>Out of Work and Nothing to Do</u>.
(photo: courtesy of the Frick Art Reference Library).

CHAPTER I

Early Days in Hudson and New York

Francis William Edmonds, 1806-1863, is most frequently identified as a cashier and part-time painter, but he preferred to state his occupation as artist when the opportunity arose. The standard reference works state that he specialized in genre, but his first eight or nine exhibited pictures were from literary sources, an interest that he sustained throughout his life. Many artists selected from literature, but the wide variety of subject matter that Edmonds chose from was most unusual. It is his work as an artist that has brought him back into the public eye, but his creativity was expressed in his business life as well, which was centered in the expanding cosmopolitanism that made New York City the intellectual and financial hub of the United States. What lends the examination of his life unusual significance was his unique ability to move freely across the lines of the artistic, cultural and financial communities of New York and to mingle with and influence its leaders.

By 1825, New York City had become the literary capital of America, its writers, magazines and publishing houses exceeding all others in number and prestige.[1] In the 1820s, there had still been a contest between Philadelphia and New York as to which would emerge as the art center of the United States, but by 1840 the contest had been decided in favor of New York. Many variables made the city attractive to artists. A significant asset lay in the generosity of patrons drawn from New York's professional and mercantile classes. The literary community offered an intellectual stimulation that held the artists and writers together. Literature had a higher status than the visual arts then, because it was free of the craft legacy that still adhered to the artists.[2] "Knickerbockers" was the name applied to the writers who wrote in Salmagundi in the second decade of the century and by 1825 it was a name given to almost any author who worked in New York.[3] These writers were established for a full decade before the artists followed the same paths. The Knickerbockers' entrenched position worked to aid the artists, because the writers were able to give the artists publicity in newspaper reviews, biographical sketches and poems of appreciation. The writers welcomed the arrival of painters and sculptors as a symbol of the growth of national taste and as a touch of the picturesque.[4]

---

1) James T. Callow, Kindred Spirits (Chapel Hill, 1967), 3.

2) Neil Harris, The Artist in American Society: The Formative Years 1790-1860 (New York, 1966), 112-114.

3) Callow, op. cit., 3.

4) Harris, op. cit., 112-114.

Edmonds came to the city in 1823, at the very beginning of its upward spiral towards art leadership in the United States.

Francis Henry William Edmonds born in Hudson, New York on November 23, 1806 was the seventh child of Samuel Edmonds and Lydia Worth. The "almost universal ambition to get forward" was expressed as early as 1815 as descriptive of the American character by Hezekiah Niles, a leading printer of his day.[5] Samuel Edmonds not only exemplified this, but passed his ambition on to his sons. Samuel joined the Revolutionary army at 16 as a private, but ended the war with the rank of assistant commissary. His end-of-the-war rewards consisted only of a horse, bridle, saddle, two blankets and a little Continental money. He settled in Hudson, then called Claverack Landing, and opened a small store. In the course of his lifetime, he sat in the state assembly and became high sheriff of the county. He continued in trade until 1812 when he reentered the army as Paymaster-General of the New York State Militia, a position he maintained for several years after the termination of the war.[6]

Lydia Worth had been a Quaker when she married Samuel Edmonds in 1786. The family likes to recall that Lydia

---

5) George Rogers Taylor, The Transportation Revolution (New York, 1951), 4.

6) William Raymond, Biographical Sketches of the Distinguished Men of Columbia County (Albany, 1851), 79.

had been "read out" of the Quaker meeting when she married
a soldier, but was readmitted upon her promise never to do
it again. This nice little story becomes suspect when we
learn that Samuel had been married first to Ruth, Lydia's
sister in 1784, but Ruth had died in childbirth within
the year. The story can be more probably applied to Ruth.
The Quaker influence of his mother, however, can be seen
in Edmonds' paintings. Francis was sent to a Quaker school
that left him with recollections of frequent reprimands
for drawing pictures upon his slate instead of doing sums
in arithmetic. Later, his Quaker schoolmaster encouraged
this propensity.[7]

His "passion for the pencil" was recalled in a number
of early anecdotes and was embodied later in a number of
paintings.[8] Soldiers were a commonplace at a Paymaster-
General's home. The first drawing Francis remembered execut-
ing was of a soldier on horseback, under which one of his
sisters had written "Captain Ketcham" for the small boy.[9]
On one occasion, Francis was punished for drawing the
teacher as he cut a ludicrous figure while holding a boy's
head between his legs for flogging. He had to submit to

---

7) Francis William Edmonds, "Autobiography" (1844),
MSS. in possession of Francis Edmonds Tyng, Clifton, New
Jersey. (There are two other versions by our author, each
of which will be indicated by Roman numerals, I, II, III),
III, 2-3.

8) Edmonds, "Autobiography," II, 1.

9) Edmonds, "Autobiography," III, 2.

the same kind of punishment.[10]

Edmonds utilized these early memories in at least three paintings. The New Scholar, a deservedly popular and highly praised picture that was also engraved by the American Art-Union, showed a reluctant boy being pushed forward by his mother as the schoolmaster hides the switch behind his back. There is a glimpse of the other pupils in the schoolroom through an open door. Despite the implied menace of the switch, this teacher does not look too forbidding. The Two Culprits, (now titled The Schoolmaster), depicts a more malicious looking fellow who grimly clutches a ruler as he faces the two culprits. The details include even the cracks in the schoolroom walls. The third painting deals with The Sleepy Student unable to keep his eyes open while he studies at home. Perhaps this last one was autobiographical. Edmonds claimed that he was no great scholar, since he preferred to spend all his leisure hours in drawing, engraving or carving.[11]

His papers bear out his assertion, for they are full of mistakes in spelling and punctuation. Some are obviously just careless, because they are right on some pages and wrong on others. Nevertheless, his detailed paintings, done with a fine brush and tight finish are painstaking and his banking reputation was built on his ability to handle

---

10) Edmonds, "Autobiography," III, 2.

11) Edmonds, "Autobiography," II, 1.

fiscal details. When his interest was involved, this force-
ful, innovative man showed his ability to achieve. His
flair for innovation is illustrated in several autobiographical anecdotes about his beginnings in art.

His material for drawing had consisted of one "led"
(sic) pencil, an eraser and a small box of water colors
with a camel's hair brush. When he tired of these, he
wanted to try his hand at oils, but in 1819 there were no
stores where one could buy artists' supplies. He went to
a house painter's store with his total capital of 25 cents.
There he spent 15 cents on five "primitive" colors in the
dry state and six cents for some oil and turpentine. He
picked up a white marble flagstone from his yard, replacing
it with a plain grey stone, and ground down the surface
of the stone with sand and water to make it smooth. On
this smooth surface, he ground his paints and when finished
poured them into improvised clam shell pots. Although
he attempted to "smooth" some canvas to make it suitable
for painting, he was unsuccessful and had to use it in its
rough state. After he had copied one or two engravings, he
decided to do a work from nature. He prevailed on one of
his friends to go with him to a small remote building on
his father's property. There, his friend posed for him by
rolling up his pantaloons, thus giving him his first opportunity to do an anatomical drawing from life. They were
discovered by a gentleman who, stumbling upon this ridiculous

scene, "bust out laughing." The story was repeated with so many variations that Francis' young friend would not pose for him again.[12]

The boy's interest and ability in drawing did not go unnoticed. The many-faceted William Dunlap was appointed Assistant Paymaster-General for the New York State Militia in 1814. The position required him to travel over the entire state in pursuance of his duties.[13] Dunlap stopped many times at the home of Paymaster-General Edmonds. Francis recalled that when Dunlap was in Hudson on one of those occasions, he saw some of the boy's drawings and went to considerable trouble to locate the shy lad to encourage him to continue. He also took Francis with him on a sketching trip to the Catskills. Shortly afterwards, an artist from Philadelphia, identified only as Cauldwell, who had also noticed Francis' artistic work, took him on a trip to Niagara Falls. Edmonds reminisced about this in 1844, "To visit these places in those years (over 30 years ago), it should be remembered was something of an undertaking to what it is now."[14] This was a reference to the transportation revolution and its impact on all Americans in Edmonds' lifetime. When Edmonds was a boy, prior

---

12) Edmonds, "Autobiography," II, 1.

13) William Dunlap, Diary of William Dunlap (3 vols., New York, 1930), I, xxii.

14) Edmonds, "Autobiography," II, 1.

to 1820, the steamboat had just become important, the Erie Canal was only under construction and the railroad belonged to the future.

Several acquaintances of Edmonds' father urged him to put the artistic bent of the boy to practical use. A correspondence was begun with Gideon Fairman of Philadelphia who was at the head of his profession as an engraver. Fairman's fee was $1000, with the additional requirement that the boy board and clothe himself. This was out of the question financially and, although several other attempts were made, nothing was done.[15] The result was that "...for about a year and a half after I left school my time was chiefly spent upon a farm about 3 miles back of Hudson and here I saw much of the rural life which afforded me so many subjects for my pictures."[16] In the fall of 1823, Gorham A. Worth, Francis' maternal uncle, then Cashier of the Tradesmen's Bank in New York City, sent for him to enter the bank as an under clerk.[17]

Edmonds' introduction to the business world came at a time of sustained economic growth. Expansion, encouraged by innovation and technological change, moved right along with only slight interruptions from minor recessions.[18]

---

15) Edmonds, "Autobiography," III, 5-6.

16) Edmonds, "Autobiography," I, 1.

17) Edmonds, "Autobiography," III, 6.

18) Taylor, op. cit., 338.

The Industrial Revolution had produced basic changes in
the economy. The attendant diversification of economic
effort, expanding utilization of credit and the spread of
the spirit of enterprise were shaking to pieces the simpler
economy of 18th century America. Enterprise had placed
such subtle instrumentalities as credit, accounting and
the corporate forms of organization at the disposal of
people unaccustomed to such things. In business, money
was giving way to promises to pay money, most of which
were never performed, but were cancelled by bookkeepers in
the offset of liabilities; and specie was dissolving into
obligations to pay specie in a volume greatly exceeding
the total that existed in the banks. Adam Smith and others
stated that a bank could legitimately put into circulation
promises to pay equal in amount to five times the gold and
silver it had in its vaults. To John Adams this seemed a
monstrous cheat and to Thomas Jefferson it was a swindle.
The majority of Americans thought so, too, but seeing how
well it worked, calmed their consciences. Probably not
one banker in four clearly understood what he was doing
and what made it sound and proper. The others could neither
intelligently explain what they were doing, nor justify it.
To an extent, therefore, they could not tell the difference
between right and wrong; if they could owe five times what
they could pay, why not a hundred?[19]

19) Bray Hammond, Banks and Politics in America
(Princeton, 1957), 274-5.

This was the confusing world into which Francis Edmonds plunged in 1823. The activities at the bank were so demanding of Edmonds' time for the first several years that he was unable to do anything else. By 1826, however, Edmonds was rooming in Pearl Street with George W. Hatch, a pupil of Durand who urged Edmonds to enroll in the newly formed National Academy of Design. Since the classes at the Antique School met at night, Edmonds was able to attend and still retain his job. Here he met William S. Mount, J.A. Adams, the wood engraver, William Page and Raphael Hoyle.[20]

Edmonds' drawings at the Academy were creditable enough to bring compliments from Samuel Morse, the president of the Academy, on several occasions. This success encouraged Edmonds to attempt an oil for the Academy exhibition. He chose a literary subject from Samuel Butler's Hudibras, entitled Hudibras Catching the Fiddler.[21] In later years, a laudatory review of an Edmonds work had the following explanation for the source of Edmonds' subject matter: "He is a man of quite extensive reading and expansive mind, and his pictures are an index to the humour which it contains."[22] It was the first oil that Edmonds had ever carefully finished and his first of an original subject. According to Edmonds,

---

20) Edmonds "Autobiography," III, 7.

21) National Academy of Design Catalogue 1829, No. 21. (Hereafter NAD).

22) American Art-Union Press Book, The New-York Historical Society, Express (New York, n.d.).

the critics had praised it and William Dunlap had lauded it extravagantly to Edmonds' friend, J.A. Adams, having mistaken the one man for the other.[23] It was on the basis of this painting that Edmonds was elected as an Associate of the Academy in 1829.[24]

The choice of a subject derived from literature indicated the impact on Edmonds of the current philosophies he faced that put history painting in the top category and realistic landscape and genre at the bottom. The nationalism that gave 19th century realistic genre painting its impetus, became a patriotic and even a radical act for some. For others, however, the jump from neo-classical history painting was too much to absorb. Here literature provided a stepping stone, because the painter was not picturing commonplace reality but was working from texts as history painters did. English genre favored Shakespeare, Sterne, Fielding and Scott. Irving supplied exoticism that could be defined as American with his tales of New Amsterdam.[25] Edmonds found suitable topics to paint on both sides of the Atlantic.

Other ideas for topics may have come to Edmonds from work that he engaged in aside from his bank position. He

23) Edmonds, "Autobiography," III, 6-7.

24) Thomas S. Cummings, N.A., Historic Annals of the National Academy of Design (Philadelphia, 1865), 116.

25) James T. Flexner, That Wilder Image (New York, 1962), 21-2.

claimed that "...I was much engaged in drawing on wood for
the engravers and was almost the only person excepting the
Rev. Henry Morton that pursued this branch of the arts in
the city..."[26] The second version of the autobiography
established that it was at the Antique School that Edmonds
met Anderson and Adams, the wood engravers who employed him
to make designs for them on their blocks. In those early
years of wood engraving, the illustrator was considered
second in importance, so that the records generally show
only the engraver's name and not who did the designs for
the wood block.[27] As a result there is no way of establish-
ing which of the early designs may have been drawn by
Edmonds.

The experience that Edmonds gained from working for
the engravers proved valuable in many ways. The drawing
on the block was excellent practice since it required him
to study composition, light, shade and drawing. It was
particularly serviceable because of the inability to alter
or erase. It also obliged Edmonds to familiarize himself
with the forms of many objects.[28] The quality of Edmonds'
drawing must have been better than adequate because other
artists would surely have been interested in a sideline that
could pay up to $15 a day, then a very substantial sum.[29]

26) Edmonds, "Autobiography," III, 7.

27) Sinclair Hamilton, Early American Bank Illustrators and Wood Engravers, 1803-1870 (Princeton, 1958), xxxv.

28) Edmonds, "Autobiography, "III, 7.

29) Ibid.

This early connection with the engraving business became a lifelong involvement that was to be a profitable source of income for Edmonds.

The art had to be put aside for several years when Edmonds was appointed Cashier of the Hudson River Bank in his native town in 1830. While there he married Martha Norman, with whom he had two children, a boy and a girl. By 1832, Edmonds was back in New York City as Cashier in the Leather Manufacturers Bank.[30] The presumption is that on his return he had gone into engraving as a business. From 1833 until 1837, there were no less than four bank note engraving companies with a "William Edmonds" in partnership with various combinations of Durand, Casilear, Gurley, Burton, Jones and Smillie.[31] It is too much of a coincidence for it to have been another William Edmonds, especially when we know that the team of Edmonds, Jones and Smillie formed the Bank Note Engraving Company after the demise of the American Art-Union. It was in these same years that Edmonds felt it necessary to exhibit his paintings under a pseudonym. He may have felt so insecure as to rule out even another business venture under his own name.

30) Cummings, op. cit., 317.

31) Sol Altmann, E.P.S. No. 25, United States Designers and Engravers of Bank Notes and Stamps (MSS, Print Room, New York Public Library, tentative date, 1961), 67; William Edmonds as listed in the City Directory from 1832-1847 appears to be F.W. Edmonds because of corresponding changes of addresses.

Neither marriage, nor the engraving business, nor a successful banking career could put an end to Edmonds' need to paint, but when he began again he ran into difficulties. Adams told Edmonds later that it had looked as if he "had forgotten the art entirely." Edmonds was dissatisfied too, but felt his problems were only mechanical. To overcome them, he went to William Page, who "was beginning to make a noise by his productions and as I was much pleased with his coloring...I employed him to paint my portrait, upon condition that he would place a looking glass behind him by which I could observe his process of commencing and finishing a head." Page not only agreed but also gave Edmonds many hints as he went along, which Edmonds would promptly commit to paper when he returned home.[32]

Page has been described as "a brilliant talker, a speculative mind, an impulsive, emotional nature...always unpredictable and controversial...(who) took up again... Allston's interest in Venetian color and monumentality, to which he added his own peculiarities."[33] It is interesting, but not surprising that Edmonds chose Page above all the other artists he knew. Color was always a major preoccupation for Edmonds and his work shows that he learned his lessons from Page very well. If Edmonds excelled in any aspect of painting, it was in his color, which was rich,

---

32) Edmonds, "Autobiography," III, 8.

33) E.P. Richardson, Painting in America (New York, 1956), 183.

varied and subtle.

Believing that he had learned something from Page, Edmonds began a small picture for the NAD exhibition of 1836. The subject, from Moore's Melodies was called Sammy the Tailor. To be sure of getting it right, he first modeled it in clay, draped it and placed it in a box to get just the light he wanted. He then worked harder upon it than on any other picture in his life. When it was finished, he would only show it to Adams because of his doubts and fears. Adams advised him to submit it. Edmonds did, but entered it under the pseudonym of E.F. Williams.[34] In the first two versions of his autobiography, he stated that the reason for the alias was the strong prejudice held by businessmen against any businessman who would devote any portion of his time to anything like poetry, painting or music. The final version, however, stated that the fictitious name had been chosen in case he would be ashamed of his painting.[35]

At the exhibition the painting was hung very low, near the floor, to Edmonds' relief, since he hoped it would escape attention. "But to my surprise for so small a work it was quite popular and sundry enquiries were made as to the whereabouts of this Mr. Williams."[36] The NAD catalogue for

---

34) Edmonds, "Autobiography," III, 9.

35) Ibid.

36) Edmonds, "Autobiography," III, 9.

1836 carried the little rhyme that went with the picture, which was exhibited as No. 225:

> Says Sammy the Tailor to me,
>   As he sat with his spindles cross-ways,
> 'Tis bekase I'm a poet you see,
>   That I kiver my head with green baize.
>   Moore's Melodies
>   (Sir Thomas Moore)

The Knickerbocker's comment was, "Good again, very good. Sammy is clearly in the full tide of inspiration and the gentleman who took his portrait has done him ample justice."[37]

The success of this venture encouraged Edmonds to continue and the following year he entered two more pictures under his pseudonym. These were also well received and praised by the critics. Adams, who could no longer withhold the real name of the artist, divulged it to several people. As a result, Edmonds was elected as Associate of the Academy for a second time in 1837.[38] During his years of inactivity, his first membership had expired.

The two paintings for 1837 were The Skinner Alarmed, and Dominie Sampson Reading the King's Commission to the Laird of Ellangowan. One critic said, "Mr. F. Williams has a good specimen in No. 239, The Skinner, and his Dominie Sampson...has very considerable merit."[39] The New York Mirror, a weekly that featured the arts, was so

---

37) The Knickerbocker, VIII (New York, July 1836), 115.

38) Edmonds, "Autobiography," III, 10.

39) The Knickerbocker, IX (June 1837), 622.

laudatory that Edmonds' election as an Associate could have been no surprise. The critic said of Dominie Sampson that, "...we understand (it) is from the pencil of an amateur artist: it reminds us of the first composition we ever saw by the lamented Newton...The Skinner is a character well known to those versed in revolutionary history. This picture is by the hand of a master. The painter has given dignity to the cow-thief and robber of the defenceless. The attitude is too fine for the scoundrel vagabond, but it corresponds well with the face."[40]

A picture in the hands of an Edmonds' relative in Connecticut has been identified as The Skinner. A bearded man is seated at a table with a sack at his feet and one hand outstretched towards a gun. His body is partially turned as he looks over his shoulder to the doorway at the rear, through which a uniformed soldier can be seen entering the hut. The Skinner was not portrayed as a completely unsympathetic character, because Edmonds never dealt in absolutes. James Fenimore Cooper described "Skinners" in The Spy as subordinate agents, employed by the Americans to annoy the enemy. They were villains, according to Cooper, but, "It was not a moment for fastidious inquiries into abuses of any description, and oppression and injustice were the natural consequences of the possession of a military power that was uncurbed by the restraints of civil

40) New York Mirror, XIV (June 10, 1837), 399.

authority."[41] These were courageous words in 1821, because
until that time anyone who had been pro-Revolution was regarded as a hero. Cooper had taken a first step towards
the reevaluation of some of the participants. As a son of
a Revolutionary veteran, Edmonds must have been raised in
a pro-Revolutionary tradition, yet he was unable to portray
the Skinner as totally evil.

This is the earliest painting by Edmonds that is still
in existence. The color is rich and subtle, accented by
bright spots. It has the first example of a color accent
used by Edmonds that we will call "Edmonds red," because
of his use of this particular shade of red, over and over
as a color accent. This early picture already features one
of the still life groups, so typical of Edmonds, in the
right foreground.

Dominie Sampson was taken from Guy Mannering or The
Astrologer by Sir Walter Scott. The incident was described
specifically, although the descriptions of the characters
were scattered throughout the story. How faithfully Edmonds
followed the book, in this instance, we have no way of knowing, because the painting is lost. The assumption, based
on the works we do have, is that it would have been quite
true to the descriptions.

Although Edmonds was elected an Associate to the Academy
under his own name, he continued to use his pseudonym in

---

41) James Fenimore Cooper, The Spy (New York, 1946),
10-11.

1838. The various versions of his autobiography give two
different reasons for the alias. Since he no longer had
any reason to be ashamed of his work, it is likely that
the prejudice of business men was the constraining factor.
Since he did not abandon the pseudonym until he changed
positions to become the Cashier of the Mechanics' Bank,
he was probably less secure in his previous place. He had
good reason to feel more secure at the Mechanics' Bank,
because they had sought him out when they were in great
difficulties.[42]

The three paintings for 1838 were The Epicure, Comforts
of Old Age, and Ichabod Crane Teaching Katrina Van Tassel
Psalmody. There were no favorable comments on these three,
but the New York Mirror made a recommendation. "If this
gentleman would paint from nature in every particular, he
would find wonderful advantage arising from it. Our young
American artists having no old masters to study, must form
a school for themselves and that school must be built upon
nature-nature carefully studied, analyzed and understood."[43]
The autobiography merely mentions the three pictures and
moves on quickly to 1839, a much more successful year.

---

42) Francis William Edmonds, Defence of Francis W.
Edmonds, Late Cashier of The Mechanics Bank Against the
Charges Preferred Against Him by Its President and Cashier
(New York, 1855), 10-11.

43) New York Mirror, XVI (June 1838), 26.

One of the last three is in the hands of an Edmonds'
descendant in California. It is probably The Epicure
(Figure 2), but we cannot be sure. Lacking the other two
pictures it is hard to know exactly what the critic had
had in mind. The surviving painting, attractive in color
and with the identifying touch of "Edmonds red," appears
to be an interesting little genre study. Henry Tuckerman
said that The Epicure and Comforts of Old Age were illustrations from Smollett and Scott, but without further
clues it is not possible to identify the scenes.[44] Edmonds may have chosen to identify these paintings as his
in his autobiography because they were listed incorrectly
in the NAD catalogue of 1838. Numbers 241 and 247, "Comforts" and "Ichabod," were credited to a nonexistent
J. Williams, instead of the mysterious E.F. Williams.[45]

The lack of favorable criticism may have wounded
Edmonds deeply, because he hurried on to 1839 and dwelled
on his efforts for that year. From this date forward, he
once again used his own name:

> ...I exhibited the "Penny Paper" and
> "Commodore Trunion & Jack Hardcastle"
> (sic). The former consisting of many
> figures and an interior was considered
> for its grouping, effect and finish

---

44) Henry T. Tuckerman, Book of the Artists (New York,
1867), 412.

45) Mary Bartlett Cowdrey, National Academy of Design
& Its Catalogues to 1860 & National Academy of Design Exhibition Records 1826-1860 (2 vols., New York, 1943), II,
210.

> superior to all my other works–It cost me
> a deal of labour as there were so many
> figures & objects brought into the picture
> all of which were painted from life, that
> it took me the whole of the summer of 1838
> to finish it–whole groups in it were painted
> in and painted out several times.[46]

The correct title in the NAD catalogue of 1839 was

Commodore Trunnion and Jack Hatchway (Figure 3), an oil

that measured 22" x 25½" and is in private hands in New

York today. The topic had been selected from The Adventures

of Peregrine Pickle by Tobias Smollett.[47] Since this paint-

ing is available, it can be compared with the author's des-

cription of the scene and the characters. Edmonds did

very well in depicting the author's intention, although

perhaps the Commodore is not as fearsome as described, but

he outdid himself in the physical surroundings. The back-

ground is similar to some done by Sir David Wilkie, but

the composition is Edmonds' own. The color too reflects

his preoccupation with it, nor did he neglect to include

the touch of "Edmonds red."

The Commercial Advertiser praised the entire exhibit

of 1839 as being far superior to the previous ones:

> A still more remarkable feature of it is
> the striking improvement evinced by many
> of the younger artists, some, whose names
> appear for the first time in the catalogue,
> having contributed works of art which in
> point of excellence tread closely on the

---

46) Edmonds, "Autobiography," III, 10.

47) Tobias Smollett, Peregrine Pickle (Oxford, 1964),
8-9.

> productions exhibited by gentlemen who
> have long been known and honored in the
> profession. Another noticeable fact is
> the high degree of talent and skill
> evinced by some of the amateur exhibitors
> ...No. 241-"The penny paper"...This is
> one of the pictures by amateurs to which
> we had reference in the first paragraph
> of this article...Another is No. 251,
> "Commodore Trunnion and Jack Hatchway."[48]

Edmonds was elected an Academician in 1840 based on the two
fine pictures he exhibited that year, Sparking (Figure 4)
and The City and Country Beaux (Figure 5), both now at the
Sterling and Francine Clark Art Museum in Williamstown,
Mass.[49] Edmonds discussed one of the problems that arose
in Sparking in his autobiography:

> I was impressed with the idea that all the
> fire or lamplight pictures that I had seen,
> seemed to be painted altogether too red-I
> had observed that none of the pictures under
> this light had ever attempted to preserve
> the cool greys that are seen by day light
> and which I thought were not lost by candle
> or fire light. I therefore endeavored to
> preserve as far as possible these peculiar
> tints so indispensable to a fine picture-
> How far I have succeeded those familiar
> with the picture can judge.[50]

Edmonds must have succeeded, because he used the same effect and technique in Taking the Census painted in 1854.

The critics recognized the entries for 1840 as super-
lative efforts. One said:

> The drawing, color, arrangement of these
> pictures are in excellent keeping...

---

48) Commercial Advertiser (New York City) April 24,
1839.

49) Edmonds, "Autobiography," III, 11.

50) Ibid.

> Edmonds...has been frequently compared to
> Wilkie. If by this be meant that he copies
> from Wilkie's pictures, it is certainly no
> compliment and very far from the truth. He
> can be compared to Wilkie in no other par-
> ticular...than in his attention to design,
> composition, light and shade. In those
> respects, he may be said to resemble Wilkie
> and it is in those respects that Wilkie
> resembles the old masters. The great
> Scottish artist is one of the few who have
> carried all the principles of the grand-
> style into the commonest subjects; and here-
> in lies the eminent merit of his works.
> Mr. Edmonds' paintings exhibit the same at-
> tention to the correct rules of taste.[51]

The highest praise a critic could give to a genre

painter was to compare him with Wilkie. William Sidney

Mount frequently drew this comparison from the critics

just as he was often compared with Edmonds. They both

painted a "City and Country Beaux." In Edmonds' version,

the young lady who holds center stage is so filled with

vitality that it seems she must have been drawn from life.

Her reality is in marked contrast to the two men who are

caricatured beyond believability. Mount's similar picture,

The Sportsman's Last Visit, is a pallid affair by compari-

son.[52] Alfred Frankenstein has said, "Mount never referred

to a woman in all his notes. His women are quite unbelieve-

able, idealized beyond belief."[53]

---

51) Knickerbocker, XVI (July 1840), 82-3.

52) Alfred Frankenstein, Painter of Rural America:
William Sidney Mount, 1807-1868 (Washington, 1968), 18.

53) Alfred Frankenstein, Lecture at the Metropolitan
Museum, July 1, 1970.

Sparking is a sentimental picture in the sense that
it has emotion, but it is not saccharine. A comparison
of portraits of Edmonds confirms the idea that the young
man in this painting is a self-portrait. According to a
descendant, the girl in the picture was the artists' first
wife and the woman in the background was his mother.[54]
There is a special poignancy in the knowledge that Martha
Norman Edmonds was already dead when the picture was being
exhibited in 1840.[55]

Edmonds had scarcely entered the paintings in the exhibit when he, "...was attacked by an illness which baffled
the efforts of all my physicians—It was a disease in the
head and which medicine seemed impossible to eradicate—
After cupping, bleeding and a severe course of medicine I
was advised to travel in the South of Europe."[56] Edmonds
himself juxtaposed the death of his wife with the NAD exhibition, but he omitted many facts that contributed to the
diagnosis of a nervous breakdown. When he took the position of Cashier for the Mechanics' Bank in 1839, the bank
was in very bad shape. The president of the bank, Shepherd
Knapp, had other interests and was unable to lift the bank

---

54) Francis William Edmonds Folder (Art Division,
New York Public Library), Letter from Cornelia C. Flagler
Schantz to Frank Weitenkampf, Dec. 7, 1920.

55) New York City Archives, "Death certificate of
Francis N. Edmonds" /Martha N. Edmonds7, (Disease: Consumption).

56) Edmonds, "Autobiography, III, 11.

from its crippled condition. Knapp's predecessor was alleged to have committed suicide. Although Edmonds saw
that it involved years of toil and the partial abandon-
ment of his painting, ambition drove him and he accepted
the appointment.[57] He also accepted the position of
Treasurer of the Apollo Association in 1839.[58] Furthermore,
his good reputation as a skilled bank examiner led to his
selection as Secretary of a committee to investigate the
conditions in the Manhattan Bank early in 1840.[59] The
final blow, the death of his wife from "consumption" in
January 1840, might not have been unexpected, but the
pressures from all of the foregoing would have felled a
lesser man. Finally, Edmonds took the advice of the doctors
and embarked for France on the 25th of November.[60]

---

57) Edmonds "Defence," 10-11.

58) Mary Bartlett Cowdrey, American Academy of Fine
Arts and American Art-Union (2 vols., New York, 1953), I,
105.

59) Fritz Redlich, History of American Business
Leaders: Part I, Men and Ideas 1781-1840: Part II, The
Molding of American Banking, Men and Ideas 1840-1910
(New York, 1951), II, 48-9.

60) Edmonds, "Autobiography," III, 12.

CHAPTER II

Travel in Europe, 1840-1841

By the 1840s so many Americans had traveled abroad and written travel books on their experiences that they often began with an apology acknowledging the plethora.[1] In 1840, a great many American artists made the trip to the Meccas of art in London, Paris and Rome. Possibly, the advent of regular steamship service across the Atlantic, initiated in 1838, had something to do with it.[2] Asher B. Durand, Edmonds' good friend, sailed for Europe on the steamer British Queen, on June 1, 1840, along with Kensett, Casiliear and Rossiter. Their journey, a pleasant one, took 17 days.[3]

Edmonds experience on the sailing ship Emerald was very different. He left Sandy Hook on the morning of November 26, 1840 and was not able to disembark at Lands End, England until the 23rd of December.[4] The ship was at

---

1) Harris, op. cit., 126.

2) Taylor, op. cit., 112.

3) John Durand, The Life and Times of Asher B. Durand (New York, 1894), 143.

4) Francis William Edmonds, "Travel Journal" (2 vols., 1840-41), MSS. in Columbia County Historical Society, Kinderhook, N.Y. All additional references to the journal in this chapter will be made without further footnoting.

the mouth of the Channel on December 15th and making no
headway when Edmonds wrote, "tedious! tedious!! tedious!!!"
He was confined to his bed with a headache and chills on
the 17th and on the 18th he noted, "Still confined to my
bed and heartily sick in body and mind...Sick enough of a
sea voyage and wished myself home." On the 20th, when the
gale was still increasing, with the ship laboring more than
at any other time during the voyage, the cabin was filled
with smoke and there were mice in his berth. It was exceedingly cold, he had a bad headache and he mourned,
"When we shall be released from our suffering Providence
alone can say, who undoubtedly has willed it for our
good."

Kensett's diary has the horrible details of Edmonds'
journey as told to him by Edmonds. The Emerald was within
one day of Lands End when a gale with heavy chopping seas
kept them in the same spot for 14 days. The ship was bound
for Havre, but Edmonds and several companions found a pilot
who was cruising for passengers and took them ashore at a
cost of $20 each.[5] The price was exorbitant but probably
worth it to the weary travelers. Edmonds experience was not
unique in the first half of the century. Similar stories
were uniformly described with pain and repugnance by many
sojourners.[6]

---

5) John Frederick Kensett, "Diary" (1840--41), MSS.
in Frick Art Reference Library, New York City.

6) Harris, op. cit., 126-8.

Edmonds' manner of keeping his journal with a minimum
of subjective reactions and frequent rephrasings, makes it
possible that he might have considered its publication as
so many others did. Although he frequently mentions his
illness, nowhere does he refer to the recent death of his
wife or the two young children at home. His banker's train-
ing, however, did result in careful accounts that enable us
to piece the story together.

He opened his journal with a list of people to write
to and he entered the dates of letters actually posted.
Sarah Norman, who headed the list, received the most letters,
seven in all. We know that she was "Miss" Norman from one
of Durand's letters that had included a message to her.[7] She
may have been either an aunt or a sister to Martha Norman
Edmonds, we do not know specifically who she was, but we
assume that she was in charge of the children while Edmonds
sought to regain his health.

Edmonds did not stint himself while abroad, because
by his own accounting of expenses, he spent an average of
$4.19 a day. This was substantially more than most visitors
to Europe spent. Wilbur Fisk, president of Wesleyan University, discovered that his total expenses for a day came
to only two dollars.[8]

---

7) Asher B. Durand Papers, (New York Public Library,
MSS. Division), A.B. Durand to John Durand, April 12, 1841.

8) Paul R. Baker, The Fortunate Pilgrims (Cambridge,
Mass., 1964), 35.

Edmonds arrived in London on December 28th after traveling by diligence, coach and boat. He began his sightseeing
at once, immediately demonstrating the hardiness that was
to characterize his stay in Europe. The itinerary that he
and his friends maintained is exhausting to read. This was
accomplished despite the drawbacks due to Edmonds' illness.
One wonders what might he have done in full possession of
his health.

Since European travel in this era was slow and cumber-
some, Americans would stay abroad for a month or even a
season. Atlantic society on both sides fulfilled its obligations with mutual acts of hospitality.[9] Not only friendly
Europeans were involved; there were also American expatri-
ates and businessmen living abroad who welcomed the visitors.
Charles Robert Leslie, artist and expatriate, who had been
a member of the Sketch Club in New York, opened doors for
Durand and Edmonds.[10]

Private collections opened like magic for many Americans, who also managed to get hold of ball invitations and
places at coronations and royal levees.[11] One of the great
collections that Leslie obtained entree to for Edmonds and
Durand was that of Mr. Sheepshanks of Blackheath, Greenwich.
This collection included just about any contemporary artist

---

9) Harris, op. cit., 125.

10) Durand, op. cit., 148.

11) Harris, op. cit., 125.

of note in England.[12] It can be seen today in the Victoria
and Albert Museum, London.[13]

Edmonds' engraving interests were apparently as strong
as ever since the very first person he chose to call on was
A.J. Mason, the wood engraver, formerly of New York. At
Wiley and Putnam's, book publishers, he saw his good friend,
G.P. Putnam, whom he saw daily during this first brief stay
in London and again on his return some months later.

By January 5th Edmonds was on his way to the continent
to continue his journey and join Durand in Italy. The trip
to Paris took two and a half days and he arrived tired,
cold and hungry. Although there were three New Yorkers at
the hotel, he retired early due to a severe headache. These
headaches and the trouble with his eyes were to persist
throughout the rest of his life, as a later diary will show.

The next morning, however, he was sufficiently restored
to go sightseeing with his friend Kensett. The latter had
been anticipating Edmonds' arrival with some anxiety.
Kensett's diary gives the first sense of the charismatic
quality of Edmonds, to be documented by others, that won
him so many friends. "...am expecting F.W. Edmonds here
every day," was the entry for December 28, 1840, followed
by January 5th, "Have seen nor heard nothing of F.W. Edmonds,
Esq-am looking for him anxiously every hour." When Edmonds

---

12) Durand, op. cit., 148.

13) William T. Whitley, Art in England, 1800-1837
(2 vols., Cambridge, 1930), II, 188.

finally did arrive on January 8th, Kensett wrote, "...I
was most heartily glad to see him and we enjoyed a couple
hours conversation..."

Kensett then introduced Edmonds to Rossiter who he had
never met before and they all went to the Long Gallery at
the Louvre. They dined at an English restaurant because,
"...Mr. E not being altogether pleased with the french
stile of getting up dinners-and as not suiting his democratic palate." After sightseeing some more, shopping and
checking on other visitors, they spent the evening in
"...conversations on various topics artistical, poetical
and social, a son of Mr. Knapp and Cole St. Leger were with
us...Retired at 12 o'clock-having spent a very delightful
afternoon and evening."[14]

The following day, the 9th, they met at the Louvre
where Edmonds was found busily inspecting the Old Masters.
Mr. Hatch and several other Americans were present, but
since Edmonds was still not feeling well they only looked
at paintings in a general way. They met again at 6 o'clock
that evening at Edmonds' hotel and had "...just got into an
interesting conversation when we were interrupted by a
whole bevy of Americans...and the tenor of discourse changed
entirely and sprees and frolicking took the place of a more
intellectual conversation. I remained until half past ten
o.c. in hopes they would leave, but then surmised no better

14) Kensett, "Diary," op. cit., Jan. 8, 1841.

chance at that hour then at 9 o.c. and I bid them good-
night and departed home..."[15]

Kensett spent Sunday, the 10th, with Edmonds and
Rossiter, but it was raining very hard, a source of considerable irritation and disappointment to Edmonds. Kensett wrote that in Edmonds' estimation, "'Sunny France'
(to use a vulgar phrase) was not what it was cracked up to
be." The next day, the 11th, Rossiter made a very clear
lifelike sketch of Edmonds' head. Edmonds mentioned sitting
to Rossiter in his journal, too, and briefly (compared to
Kennsett's account) mentioned attending the Welles ball.
Kensett described it in detail:

> (We) were landed among a vast concourse
> of splendid equipages at the grand en-
> trance of the wealthy bankers mansion.
> We were borne upstairs. When arranging
> our dress we discovered our names were
> severally trumpeted forth as made our
> ingress to the reception room one by one,
> where the little Yankee money changer with
> his queenly spouse stood to receive their
> guests. We passed in amid the brilliant
> throng collected together in conversational
> groups or promenading. In trying to dis-
> cern the quality and quantity of beauty
> that was congregated around-Messrs. E, L
> and self took a quiet nook where we could
> observe what was going on without being
> observed while R sauntered among the guests
> in search of Healy and such others as were
> known to him. There present a goodly num-
> ber of Americans...The display of beauty
> was meager enough and did not tell flatter-
> ingly for our fair country women...There
> was a display of wealth which it seemed
> was to take the place of natural advantages
> inasmuch as many of them possessed the one
> without the other...The scene was indeed

---

15) Kensett, "Diary," _op. cit._, Jan. 9, 1841.

> a gorgeous one and made quite an affect-
> ing appeal to us ragged followers on the
> Muse. The table was supplied with all the
> luxuries that a voluptuary and gourmand
> could desire...E and L becoming weary of
> this exhibition bid us adieu about 11 o.c. [16]

Kensett described how he spent the evening of the 13th
with Edmonds. "...A most delightful evening...full of interest and practical usefulness...he related to me much of
his experience during the period of his clerkship and progress toward the position he now occupies in society-It
was teeming with excellent examples." The following day,
Kensett accompanied Edmonds through the Louvre. "We
walked along...enjoyed his remarks on the various productions of the old masters-He is much delighted with Metzu's
works and all the Dutch school-the coloring of Rubens-says
he cannot feel Titian & very few of the Italian school-of
the Spanish he prefers Murillo." [17]

Edmonds attended another affair that did not include
the other artists. This affair was given by the Minister
to France, Governor Lewis Cass, who had been the Secretary
of War in Jackson's cabinet. Edmonds left his letters with
the Minister on January 9th and presumably identified himself as a banker and Democrat on that occasion. The party
on the 14th included many "distinguished characters" some
of whom were foreign ambassadors.

---

16) Kensett, "Diary," op. cit., Jan. 11, 1841.

17) Ibid., Jan. 14, 1841.

Edmonds left Paris on January 16th with carriage and
courier and arrived in Marseille on January 21st. A letter
to Kensett said, "My journey from Paris to Marseille was
much more agreeable than I anticipated-The weather was
pleasant, the roads good and we travelled like nabobs-at
a heavy expense however, and with a rascal for a courier."[18]
In Marseille, he met Mr. Cutting and his family who were
waiting for the steamer to take them to Italy. Cutting
was an acquaintance from New York, so that the six days
they had to wait for the mistral to abate was passed with
pleasant company.[19] As they strolled the streets together,
they were struck by the cleanliness of the city and the
beauty of its streets and houses.

As a result of the dealings for transportation and
passports, Edmonds excoriated the French system of manag-
ing steam boats and everything else that related to travel
vehicles and especially, "...their agents generally great
rogues." The Mediterranean trip, however, was pleasant,
interesting and leisurely, affording opportunities for dis-
embarking to sightsee along the way. They landed at
"Citaveccia" on January 31st where Edmonds took off for
Rome.

Durand had been waiting impatiently. He wrote to his
wife that due to the news that Edmonds was on his way he

---

18) John Frederick Kensett Papers (New York State
Archives, Albany), F.W. Edmonds to Kensett, Feb. 10, 1841.

19) Ibid.; Kensett, "Diary," op. cit., Jan. 8, 1841.

had put off writing, "...in the joyful hope of seeing him daily...but as he has not yet arrived and may not for some time, I defer it no longer." The warmth of feeling that Kensett had expressed was repeated and amplified by Durand in this letter and others. He went on, "I begin to fear Edmonds will not reach here as it is bad travelling in winter from London or Paris, wherever he may be, the more so as his health is bad, but I hope he may come as his presence would be the most welcome sight in Rome."[20]

The reunion was on February 1st and they filled the day with talk and a visit to Edmonds' banker. The next day he went to see St. Peter's, along with Durand and Casilear. His journal states that the afternoon was spent in drawing from a young Italian girl in Durand's studio, but the February 10th letter to Kensett explained that she was a naked Italian girl. This is just another small indication that Edmonds thought that the journal might be meant for other eyes. The letter to Kensett contained an excuse for not writing that also hinted that Edmonds was given a royal welcome all around. "...I have been so occupied in getting settled and _Lyonizing_ that have had scarcely a moment to think, much less to _write_." It is not clear who was being lionized.

Edmonds continued to "rest" with the same frenzy that characterized his usual routines. Tourist activities and

---

20) Durand Papers, op. cit., A.B. Durand to Mary Durand, Jan. 15, 1841.

the comments about them are to be found on almost every page. Edmonds health improved slowly. The letter to Kensett said that he was about the same as in Paris, but when Durand wrote to his wife on the sixth of March, Edmonds had improved a great deal.

Among the tourist activities, there were the special attractions for the artists of the galleries, great art sights and visits to the studios of sculptors and artists working in Rome. Edmonds quickly formed the opinion that Rome was good only for painters who were aiming at the "Grand Style," but for no others and that Paris was the best place to copy pictures. "Sculptors, however, have a rich treat here and here they should always be."

The remark on sculptors was prompted by a visit to the studios of Thomas Crawford and Bertel Thorwaldsen. When Crawford arrived in Rome in 1835, he was received warmly by Thorwaldsen and given a place to work in his studio. Crawford was joined there by James E. Freeman and Luther Terry, both painters, and Crawford's studio then became another nucleus of American artist life.[21] Edmonds saw Terry often and was a frequent visitor at the studio. On this first visit, Crawford's rooms were closed, but Thorwaldsen's work made a profound impression.

Sketching as an activity was carried on by all the artists. Durand's March 6th letter to his wife said,

21) Baker, op. cit., 133.

"Edmonds has painted a little with me in my studio and done exceedingly well, but his head is not sufficiently strong to venture much..." Painting was clearly regarded as more strenuous than sketching, for Edmonds mentioned sketching as early as February 6th.

There was playtime for the artists too, even though their journals and letters made it seem quite circumspect. Edmonds' February 10th letter to Kensett had said, "Next Saturday the Carnival commences and we are all on tiptoe to see it." His journal of the 13th described the Corso crowded with people in masks and the balconies hung with festoons. For the next ten days there were remarks about the queer scenes, tomfoolery, sugar-plums and horse-racing. There was hard pelting with sugar plums and masked young women cutting all kinds of capers. They were stationed on a balcony in the Corso on the third day when one of the race horses fell and rolled into the crowd. One man was killed while stopping the horses. On the last day the Corso was lit with 10,000 candles. Durand described it to his wife, "...lighted candles...from every window and balcony, from the roofs of the houses on each side to the ground, so that the whole air seemed thickened with glittering stars, while the chief charm of the whole business consisted in the endeavor to extinguish each others lights...Edmonds and myself joined in the sport, occupying with some other Americans one of the balconies..."[22] These reactions were typical of

22) Durand Papers, op. cit., A.B. Durand to Mary Durand, Mar. 6, 1841.

most Americans who usually responded enthusiastically to
the public festivities at carnival time and periodically
the rest of the year.[23]

Durand drew a delightful picture of the improvements
in his domestic situation upon the advent of Edmonds:

> We have been constantly together, and I
> know you will rejoice with me in the
> fortunate event of his coming, even if
> he keeps me a few weeks longer from home...
> Since he has been here I have abandoned my
> barn like studio during the evenings, for
> the social comforts of his apartments. We
> in fact live together, make our own break-
> fast and tea, having the apparatus furnished
> by our landlady or Padrona, we procuring
> our own tea, bread, butter, etc, so that
> I have felt during the time that he has
> been here more like a social being enjoy-
> ing intercourse with his own kind, than at
> any time since I left my own loved home.
> You would laugh to see us boiling our tea-
> kettle, occasionally upsetting it over the
> hearth and carpet (for his room has a car-
> pet which the servant girl says cost 50
> dollars) then dishing out our tea...[24]

According to Edmonds' journal, the long days of sightseeing and shopping continued and, as the weather improved,
sightseeing was combined with sketching. A two day trip
to Tivoli, for example, resulted in many sketches for all
the artists. Another activity for Edmonds was to sit for
his portrait to a number of different artists. Rossiter
had begun one in Paris, Durand produced one that is at the
NAD today. Saulini, a gem cutter who specialized in cameo

23) Baker, op. cit., 112.

24) Durand Papers, op. cit., A.B. Durand to Mary
Durand, Mar. 6, 1841.

portraits, produced still another believed to be one held by a private collector on Long Island.[25]

Yet another activity was the shopping for oil paintings to take home. Edmonds was struck with the way copies of originals were being turned out in wholesale lots with little fidelity to the original, indicating that little has changed in Italy over the years. Even then there were government inspectors who were supposed to prevent the old masters from being taken out of the country. The shopper was supposed to content himself with second and third rate masters.

Edmonds, Durand, Casilear and a young artist, identified only as Kennedy, took a month long trip to the south of Italy. According to John Durand, his father not only regarded the whole tour as exile, to be gotten through with as soon as possible, but that Durand was not fond of all travel because its business details worried him.[26] As a general observation this was probably true, but specifically, the trip to the south had Edmonds to handle the business details. Indeed, Edmonds put a different complexion to all of Durand's feelings, as he said in a letter to his wife, "...I ought to submit with cheerfulness and thanksgiving when I reflect how desolate I should have felt, alone

25) E. Benizet, "T. Saulini," in Dictionnaire des Peintres, Sculpteurs, Dessinateurs et Graveurs (11 vols., France, 1954), VII, 534.

26) Durand, op. cit., 164.

and unfriended, as must have been my condition had I not
met this same good friend and companion, Edmonds."[27]

The trip took them to Naples, Pompeii, Herculaneum,
Paestum and other places. A return trip by boat to Naples
from Sorrento evoked a diatribe from Edmonds:

> ...distance across the Bay about 18 miles
> and such a ferry boat!!! Lazy, Lousey,
> Flea bitten, ragged seasicken & Garlic
> smelling set of ragamuffins no eye did
> ever see before-at least 60 souls on
> board a mere row boat, with not room
> enough to move one's feet-Priests, sailors,
> market women, beggars, wenches, boys no
> britches and girls with no smocks-However
> after a 6 hours sail or rather floating
> and rowing, reached Naples-got our dinner
> shook off the fleas, & set out for the
> Museum-but found it closed.

The next day they did all the tourist things on Mount
Vesuvius, observed the lava and sulphur, roasted eggs and
stayed at the top for about half an hour, during which time
Edmonds made a hasty sketch. On their way back to Naples
they met the "Royal Family" on their way to Vesuvius.
Edmonds mentioned royalty in many contexts and many times
without ever identifying which royal family was involved.
Like many democrats, however, he seemed impressed by them.

Since all four men on the trip were artists, it was
devoted to sketching combined with sightseeing all the way.
Even on the three day journey back to Rome, they made stops
to sketch. The impetus of this orgy of drawing was carried
over into the first few days back in Rome.

---

27) Durand Papers, op. cit., A.B. Durand to Mary
Durand, May 4, 1841.

The first two weeks in April were to be their last in Rome, but they delayed their departure so that they might view the ceremonies for Holy Week. The pilgrims began to pour into Rome on April 3rd, the day before Palm Sunday. On Palm Sunday, despite the stormy weather they went to St. Peter's to see the blessing of the Palms. April 8th was another impressive day with the most imposing ceremonies performed by the Pope as he blessed the multitudes, washed the pilgrim's feet and then fed them in one of the adjoining rooms. Edmonds did not fail to mention the names of some of the nobility present. He also thought the immense crowd attending caused great inconvenience.

The Easter Sunday ceremonies were as impressive as the crowds of people there to witness them. They returned in the evening to see the illumination of St. Peter's, a sight Edmonds found stirring:

> A complete outline of the church from the
> ball on the steeple to the ground was formed
> of lights and remained so till 8 o'clock,
> when of a sudden, in a twinkling of the eye
> the whole church underwent an entire change
> and presented one of the most gorgeous
> sights I ever beheld; balls of fire seem to
> pass like meteors in every direction till
> the whole was one blaze of fire; which
> lasted some 10 minutes, when they sank into
> a more star like form and left the church
> looking like a castle of the air.

By the 13th of April they had left Rome to begin the journey that was to take them back to London. In the important cities like Florence, Venice, Milan, Geneva and Paris they would stay several days or more. The first stop was Florence.

Their stay in Florence was a hectic one. They visited Hiram Powers and Shobal Vail Clevenger, sculptors, the first day, the 17th. The nucleus of American society revolved around Powers, who, in addition to welcoming visitors to his studio, entertained at his home each Wednesday evening.[28] Clevenger had enjoyed such great success in the United States as a portrait sculptor that Nicholas Longworth sponsored his trip to Italy. Unfortunately, he developed consumption and was buried at sea while returning home in 1843.[29] Present, too, was a young American painter, Nichols, who was probably Abel Nichols.[30]

The next day, in company with a group of American artists, Edmonds and Durand started the day with a stroll through the Boboli gardens. The artists were identified as Clevenger, Nichols, Kellogg and Charles, who cannot be pinpointed. Kellogg was most likely Miner Kilbourne Kellogg who was in Italy at that time.[31] They all continued around the town, met the Grand Duke and his family and then, in the afternoon, were entertained by the American consul who gave

---

28) Baker, op. cit., 56.

29) George C. Groce and David H. Wallace, Dictionary of Artists in America 1564-1860 (4th ed., New Haven, 1969), 132.

30) Ibid., 470-1.

31) Ibid., 364.

them an interesting historical talk on Florence.

The visits to the Uffizi and Pitti palaces were described by Edmonds as "a fine treat." He objected, however,
to the exhibition of the Venus di Medici in the same room
with fine paintings, because if shown by itself, like the
Apollo, it could be seen to better advantage. They ended
the day with a visit to Greenough's studio with no comment
other than the names of a few pieces of sculpture.

Edmonds passed an entire day in the "old palace" copying and making memorandums from pictures. Later, in his
banker's role, he assisted a Mr. Dixon in obtaining funds
by endorsing Dixon's draft on Rothschild. The days in
Florence continued in the same vein, but another visit to
Powers' studio resulted in a long conversation.

The discussion concerned Powers' statue of "Eve." It
was compared with the Venus di Medici without Edmonds
clarifying who was making the comparison. It seems likely
that it was Powers, because errors were pointed out in the
Venus particularly in the knees, through the back, the
length of the leg from the knee to the ankle and also in
the ankle bone. Powers then bemoaned the inadequacy of
his charges for a bust ($400) towards defraying his ex-
penses, as his head workman alone cost him $2 a day. Never-
theless, Powers was never to return home, because his work
was so in accord with the current canons of taste that the
orders flowed in.[32]

---

32) Baker, op. cit., 131.

Not everyone however, cared for Powers or his work. Henry P. Leland in Americans in Rome described an American sculptor named Chapin who was a thinly veiled portrait of Hiram Powers. Leland accused Chapin of being no more than a mass producer of so-called art.[33] There was justification for this attack, but it could have been applied to many sculptors of the era who never laid a finger to the marble, but only produced the plaster model. As Hawthorne reported in The Marble Faun, there were mechanics who, when presented with the plaster cast by the sculptor and a block of marble, "...in due time, without the necessity of his touching the work with his own finger, he will see before him the statue that is to make him renowned..."[34]

They left Florence on the 23rd of April and went on to the next major stop, Venice where they stayed for three days. They went gallery hopping, sightseeing and tried to capture the picturesque scenes of Venice in sketches. They resumed their journey, Edmonds listing everything along the way, adding an occasional clarification as he did in Verona. "The women of this place very beautiful-their long black veil, over their dark hair and fair complexions-with their fine forms and graceful movements-richly entitle them to occupy the native city of Juliet." This kind of comment was so rare for Edmonds that it is easy to forget that he

---

33) Harris, op. cit., 234-5.

34) Nathaniel Hawthorne, The Marble Faun (New York, 1961), 89.

was only 34 years old when he made this journey. He added,
"The only drawback upon Verona is the immense herds of
soldiery..." This would have been a common enough reaction
for most Americans.

They reached Milan on the 3rd of May after traveling
all night, but their exhaustion did not deter them from
taking a "commissioner" and setting out at once to examine
the city. Edmonds deplored the decayed condition of the
Last Supper by Da Vinci, mentioned various places of interest and the strange appearance of the women with their
swollen necks, supposed to be a consequence of the water.
As usual, they visited both the contemporary and historical
exhibitions of painting.

Edmonds gave a harrowing account of their passage
through the Simplon Pass on May the 6th. They started at
10 P.M. in the "Mal Poste" for Geneva with a Frenchwoman,
her two children, Durand, "K" and Edmonds. They traveled
by moonlight until midnight when they were compelled to
abandon their carriage and change with their luggage into
a one horse open wagon. They were held up by the after
effects of an avalanche, passed through several tunnels,
one of snow, over bridges thrown across torrents with the
strange and awful appearance of the mountains with the moon
just touching their tops compounding their feelings of the difficulties in the increasing cold. About a half an hour after
they reached Simplon daylight dawned and they stopped for

coffee. Now they proceeded in a small open wagon drawn by
three horses in tandem, but soon had to abandon the wagons
for sleighs. At one point their passage was so hazardous
they had to get out of the sleighs to rescue one horse from
a depth and to keep another from sliding off the road down
the mountain. They passed the Hospice about 9 A.M. where
they saw the monks, their dogs and workmen endeavoring to
clear the roads. "At one place had to forsake terra firma
entirely and go on the crust of an old avalanche over an
immense precipice to proceed..." They finally reached the
foot of the mountains at noon, but rested only two hours.

They left Briga where they had been resting and pushed
on in a diligence along the valley of the Rhone, "...offer-
ing continued change from the grand and sublime to the
picturesque and beautiful." The little town of "Sion,"
reached at 9 P.M. had been intended for them to stay all
night, but it offered so little comfort that they pushed
on to "St. Maurice" where they went to bed for two brief
hours. At 5 A.M. they left by diligence to arrive at
Villeneuve just in time to catch the steamboat at 10 A.M.
They did not reach Geneva until 4 P.M. but nothing daunted,
had dinner, "trotted out" to visit the Promenade for a view
of Mont Blanc, but it was lost in the clouds. Since they
were tired that evening they went to bed early.

The next morning Durand and Edmonds went down the
Rhone in quest of scenery to sketch, but found nothing to

please them. In the afternoon, they paid a visit to Vol-
taire's residence where among other items of interest they
noticed two pictures of Franklin and Washington. On their
return, they had a fine view of the mountains with the exception of Mont Blanc still hidden by clouds. The following morning they were able to make their sketches of Mont
Blanc.

In the afternoon, they went to the art gallery and
then to the Protestant burying ground where they were
shocked by the practice of destroying the graves after 15
years burial and scattering the bone ashes to the winds.
It was a very pretty place with each grave planted with
flowers, many in full bloom. From there they went to the
Cathedral in the, "hopes of beholding the pulpit from which
Calvin sent forth his denunciations against a good-natured
world." The only day the Cathedral was open was on Sunday,
the first such experience since Edmonds had been abroad.

They left Geneva at 10 P.M. on May 11th, again riding
all night, something Edmonds did not find agreeable. Nor
did he care for what he regarded as the unnecessary examination of their persons and baggage when they crossed the
French line. They reached Lyons at 8 A.M. on the 12th and
this ended Edmonds first book. The last pages had a list
of expenses with the notation that it would be carried to
Volume II. The facing page had a water color drawing of
some figures around a large pot on an open fire.

After spending a day in Lyons, they resumed their
journey and arrived in Paris on May 15th. They immediately
dressed and went out to look up their friends. Kensett
had only been notified of their impending arrival that
very day and was therefore very much astonished to find
Durand and Edmonds at his door. Edmonds was hardly recog-
nisable for he now sported a ferocious pair of black
mustachios. Edmonds made no mention of this in _his_ journal.
Kensett made an enlightening comment here that may explain
some aspects of the hectic journey from Rome. "Mr. Durand
as usual ready to carry business and pleasure at a loco-
motion speed..."[35] We know that Edmonds was no slouch, but
John Durand projected a very different picture of his
father.

They talked for several hours and then Kensett accompanied them to the tailors for coats and "pantaloons."
After calling upon a German artist, unnamed, they went in
search of hats. At first they were unable to "...find a
chapeau of sufficient dimensions for the ponderous tete
of Mr. Edmonds..." but eventually succeeded. At their
hotel, Kensett was shown their sketches, many of which,
though hasty were exceedingly fine. He particularly liked
Durand's sketch of Mont Blanc that he called varied and
picturesque and thought that it would paint well. He commented on Edmonds' work: "On the whole Mr. Edmonds efforts

---

35) Kensett, "Diary," _op. cit._, May 15, 1841.

were distinguished by greater boldness and character, though
they may have been less true-there is a vigor as well as
agreeable arrangements of lines and objects that gives them
in my humble opinion an evident superiority."[36]

Kensett's criticism of Durand's portrait of Edmonds
is valid because we not only have the picture in question
at the NAD (Figure 6), but many self-portraits to compare
it with. Kensett said, "...Durand's portrait of Edmonds
quite disappoints me. It looks tame and more like a lump
of flesh than a portrait of F.W. Edmonds."

Edmonds gained permission to copy paintings in the
Louvre. This may have been difficult to obtain, since
Edmonds mentioned how convenient and important it was for
an artist to have his profession listed on his passport
for permission to paint in the Louvre for eight months.
Edmonds' profession was not listed in his passport, which
still exists. Copying at the Louvre was allowed only on
Tuesdays, Wednesdays, Thursdays and Fridays, from 9 A.M.
to 4 P.M. The door-keeper supplied the easel and those who
were first on line had the choice of situation.

When they weren't painting, or shopping for clothes,
or sightseeing, they were shopping for prints and engravings at the Louvre on the Boulevards. By the 28th of May,
Kensett commented that both Edmonds and Durand had made
very clever collections of prints, considering their limited

---

36) Kensett, "Diary," op. cit., May 15, 1841.

stay, that would doubtless form valuable acquisitions to
their studios. "Their copies as far as gone on with are
certainly excellent-That is Metsus and Terburgs-Edmonds
has made several sketches in water colours and oil bases
which will serve a good purpose."[37] At least one of the
water colors is held by a relative of Edmonds on Long
Island.

By the 31st of May, they had left Paris and once again
Edmonds' diary is filled with place names as they hurried
along. He admired the Cathedral in Rouen for being the
best specimen of Gothic architecture that he had seen in
France or Italy. He also liked the antiquated appearance
of those houses and streets in Rouen that retained more of
the look of the Middle Ages than any he had seen elsewhere.

Arrival in London was on June 3rd and Edmonds began
a virtual orgy of examining art of the past and present.
His discussions of art and artists will be reserved for
the next chapter, but some of his experiences are worth
reporting. "...Hyde Park-extensive affair; but not as
picturesque as I expected-little else than a large grazing
field-The rides around it however are very fashionable and
crowded..."

The respect shown to Sunday in London presented an
even more forbidding aspect than New York on a Sunday and
a very different one from the Continent where there was

---

37) Kensett, "Diary," op. cit., May 28, 1841.

hardly any change from a weekday. "...all this is perhaps as it should be; we who have been educated in the land of steady habits ought not to murmur at the respect shown to Sunday in England. The only fear in this respect is only external, as the Londoners are famous for excursions and fine dinners on Sunday, and consider attendance once a day at church quite sufficient for the whole week." If Edmonds was in the habit of attending church more frequently than once a week in the 40s, he must have changed, because by 1854 his diary reports church attendance as once a week, on Sunday.

Edmonds' view of John Bull in every variety of shape, style and condition was that some of the gentry were fine looking fellows, but the ladies fell short of expectation. He was also surprised to learn that London was growing as fast as any city in the New World, an evidence of some American provincial pride.

Chance took Edmonds to the Ascot Races, or so he says. He had not been at the race course many minutes when Queen Victoria arrived escorted by Prince Albert, accompanied by many of the nobility and gentry. Victoria appeared to be "...very plain and comely personage, rather short, with an ordinary but pleasant look. Her manners were also plain and likewise her dress-In short I should have supposed her to be the wife of some comfortable young tradesman had I not known to the contrary-Prince Albert is also quite ordinary-rather diffident and retiring, with nothing bright

in his countenance-The ladies would call him 'good-look-
ing.'"

The race course presented the greatest and the lowest
in the land, from Queen to beggar along with gambling in
its worst features. "Ladies of the highest rank putting
down sovereign after sovereign at the Roulette tables-
Then the eating, drinking, and betting!-money changed hands
in the thousands as though it was mere sawdust...the animals
and riders were in beautiful order and this part of the
days entertainment certainly worth viewing."

Leslie was once again very kind to the visiting artists,
procuring an unusual invitation for them to visit inside
Buckingham Palace where he was engaged on a painting of
the Baptism of the infant princess. Leslie described to
them how he had been admitted to the throne room while the
baptismal ceremony was in progress so he could draw the
scene on the spot. Edmonds' journal exclaims over the
splendid furniture and rooms, but the group's main target
was the painting gallery. This was the last day spent with
Durand who was leaving for New York.

Edmonds remained in England in order to make a trip
to the north of England and Scotland. He started on the
18th of June and the "country presented a complete picture
every mile of the way-England is, so far, really a Garden."
Birmingham, reached later the next day, was similar in
appearance to the east side of New York City. The late
hour did not discourage Edmonds from taking off that very

evening for Stratford-on-Avon to see the house where
Shakespeare was born and the church where he was buried.
Not the least curiosity was the immense number of names
inscribed on the wall, windows and chairs, including those
of Sir Walter Scott, Schiller and Washington Irving. The
next morning he arose at 5 A.M. with the intention of
getting a sketch of the church where Shakespeare was
buried, from a river vantage point, but had to wait until
later in the day, because no one else was up yet.

By noon, they (apparently Edmonds had a companion not
named) were packed and off by private carriage to Warwick
where they stopped at "Swan Inn." From a good vantage
point at the windows they had a view of people returning
from church. Edmonds' Quaker upbringing caused him to
notice, "...The Quakers particularly riding in splendid
carriages with servants in Livery." They found Warwick
very picturesque and well worth their visit. Its good
order made a strong contrast with the magnificent pile of
Gothic ruins of Kenilworth. Officially destroyed by Crom-
well, its owner had taken great pains to preserve the ruins.
The portions of the original ceiling, doors and mantle
pieces in oak from the old castle that were preserved in
their antiquated state were quite new to Edmonds.

A trip from Liverpool to Glasgow was made by steamer.
Edmonds made some cryptic notes on this occasion that one
could wish he had expanded. "...passengers-character dis-
played-attention bestowed upon a negro-its effect upon us-

American prejudice-etc." They hurried through Glasgow on
their way to Edinburgh. The latter struck Edmonds as one
of the most beautiful cities in Europe and reminded him
of Martin's fine pictures. Its people delighted in exhibiting their city, while the writings of Sir Walter
Scott had added to its charm.

In fact, the visit to Abbotsford, the residence of
Sir Walter Scott, had to be one of the main reasons for
the trip to Scotland. It had to be reached from Melrose,
the nearest town three miles away, but owing to a Fair in
the neighboring town there was no carriage available.
Nothing daunted, they set off on foot. Scott had been a
source of subject matter for paintings by Edmonds and his
reverential attitude can be evinced by the careful and
lengthy account of the tour through Abbotsford. Afterwards,
they returned to Melrose along the river bank in time to
visit the Old Abbey there. Edmonds wrote, "Truly these
old ruins are worth a voyage across the Atlantic to see;
unless the person should be like my companion who thought
them a mere pile of rubbish." It was here that Sir Walter
loved to linger, and truly they excite feelings not akin
to every day matters." The day was completed with a trip
to Dayburgh Abbey that was made possible when a carriage
became available. Here Edmonds had another treat inspecting the ruins and grave of Sir Walter that he described
in detail.

They left Melrose that same evening and several days
later, July 2nd they arrived in Manchester with Edmonds
so ill that he was obliged to call on the apothecary for
medicine. He moaned in his journal, "How dreary it is to
be unwell in a foreign land among strangers! Oh, for the
ministering hand of some kind female! But this is denied
me."

Although the doctor advised Edmonds to remain in bed
for a day, his impatient companion hurried them off to
catch the train for Birmingham at 6 A.M. Edmonds arrived
alone, his companion having remained some 50 miles back
at another station with no reason given. Feeling somewhat
better, he strolled through the city in the afternoon.
His observations were similar to many Americans of his day
about the destiny of the U.S.:

> It being Saturday afternoon, the workmen
> had been paid off, and the streets were afloat
> with a dense mass of human flesh. But their
> appearance was anything but flattering-They
> looked sickly, dirty and ragged-The gin shops
> were filled with men and women-and beggars
> and miserable objects of human deformity
> filled up the picture-Mountbanks, showmen
> and trafficers of small ware, were loud in
> their cries to gain a penny-peddling letter
> paper '6 sheets for a penny' 'head acts for
> two pennys' and an exhibition of Rope dancers
> addmittance 'one penny'-I saw enough to hope
> that our country will be agricultural rather
> than a manufacturing nation-multitudes of
> human beings confined day after day in closely
> walled rooms is not the thing to produce
> bodily or mental strength.

This rather grim view accurately portrayed England in that
phase of its capitalism.

The fourth of July was underlined and followed with
three exclamations marks in the diary. "This is the anni-
versary of our independence and Americans never appreciate
it more than when abroad among strangers in a strange
land." It was Sunday, so he "attended service...heard a
preacher of considerable reputation in this quarter; and
was surprised to find in an <u>English Established Church</u> such
bold & fearless language-He was an able man, but rather
determined to frighten than persuade his hearers into religious feeling..."

He arrived in London the next day with but 10 days
left to spend in England. The many letters waiting for
him from friends and family in America and Paris reported
that all were well. Now the room in London felt like home
and he was glad to be back in it. That same evening he sat
down to enter his thoughts on his tour now that it was
virtually at its end. He started with, "<u>What benefit after
all has it been to me</u>?" (his underlining). His health,
though not totally restored was greatly improved and he had
gained much knowledge of customs and people. Moreover, he
had, "...shaken off, in a great measure, a foolish feeling
of diffidence which has accompanied me through life, and a
longing for loneliness and a preference for my own society
which has tended to create moroseness, sourness and a re-
pining at the lot Providence has assigned me-I have also
learned to control my ambition and to be content with doing
less for mere reputation sake, and more for my present

comfort and happiness...I have found that for the first
time in my life I could leave my business behind me and
scarcely give it a passing thought for the space of seven
months!!"

All of this from a young man who had met with great
success, not only in his business life, but in his chosen
avocation. This picture of himself is greatly at odds
with those seen through other eyes. Yet, his breakdown
had been real enough and the symptoms which followed that
resemble anxiety symptoms never left him.

He continued to see and do things right up until his
departure. At the Gallery of Practical Science, he saw some
interesting experiments on electricity and polar light.
He made the rounds of his London friends to say goodbye and
did some last minute shopping. He went by train to Bristol,
his embarkation point, where he saw a "...famous Iron steamer
now being built." This steamer was destined to revolution-
ize shipping. Edmonds described it. "This steamer is to
be propelled by the Archimedes screw-she is 3,000 tons-300
feet long, and is really a wonder of the kind." This was
probably the first large ship to combine the two new prin-
ciples, the iron hull and the screw. It most likely was
the Great Britain that was under construction and made its
first crossing from Liverpool to New York in 1845. It was
not until 1860 that its superiority gained recognition.[38]

---

38) Taylor, op. cit., 118.

The steamers that crossed the Atlantic until that time were propelled by the paddle wheel.

Edmonds' return journey was made in a steamer, the Great Western. The trip took half the time the sailing ship had taken to come the other way, but even on this voyage there were some storms that made travel uncomfortable.

Edmonds closed his second book with a self-portrait seated at the table, head on hand, eyes closed and a glass on the table. A more fitting end to his journal would be Edmonds' resolutions made when he completed his self-assessment. He asked himself if he could keep his regained health and would the knowledge gained abroad be of real service in the future? His answer was:

> It is certain that if I restrain my ambition and not be too anxious to do too much: be patient; take things easily; allow nothing to fret me; submit to the changes and chances of fortune with perfect good nature; mingle freely with society; avoid being too much alone; use every convenient opportunity by reading books of travel to refreshen my impression of the countries thro' which I have passed; paint but little and rather for pleasure than reputation; finally think slowly, work slowly, eat slowly and walk slowly, I shall get a good appetite, sleep soundly, digest well, and live happily-and good health must follow as a matter of course-But the great question remains to be asked-namely-Can I do all this? my reply shall be like the brave Miller's "I WILL TRY." and may God assist me in the same.

CHAPTER III

Art Criticism and Comparisons

By the time Edmonds made his trip abroad, not only was his style formed, but he had developed strong ideas on art in general. Some of the latter were modified as a result of the experience, but there was no basic change in his style. His journal was filled with his reactions from brief notes to lengthy dissertations. As might be expected, his views often coincided with those of his contemporaries and other artistic opinions then in print, but they also disagreed in a highly individual way. He was obsessed with color and how it was made and this always affected his final reaction to a work of art where color was involved.

The American artist who went to Europe at this time had the advantage of viewing art from a relatively unprejudiced background. At this time, in America, there was nothing like the war in France between the romanticists and neo-classicists led by Delacroix and Ingres.[1] There was, however, an esthetic ideal that was held by most American artists in common. This will develop from an analysis of Edmonds' critical ideas.

1) Richardson, op. cit., 215.

Edmonds and Asher B. Durand had reacted to their first views of the "Old Masters," in 1840, with disappointment. Durand might have communicated his feelings to Edmonds by letter, since he came to London six months earlier, but each man had different preferences. Durand said that only Rubens, Murillo, Van Dyck, Rembrandt, Both, Cuyp and Salvator Rosa surpassed his expectations.[2] Edmonds selected only Wilkie, Reynolds and Lawrence.[3] Their experience was quite different from that of the average American tourist who was overcome by what Europe had to offer in the arts.[4]

Edmonds' initial visit to the Louvre gave him the opportunity to make an assessment of what it had to offer. He noted that it would take months to be seen to advantage. He had been in Rome but a short time when he wrote to Kensett that Paris was undoubtedly the best place for copying and that Rome was the place for those painters who were aiming at the grand style, but none others. The same letter spoke of Raphael, "...I admire most in his frescos-His Transfiguration is good but not equal in my opinion to his School of Athens."[5] Edmonds came to value Michelangelo above Raphael. On March 7th he said, "Had another specimen

---

2) Durand , op. cit., 147.

3) Edmonds, "Travel Journal," (As in the preceding chapter, unless otherwise noted, all material is from the journal and will not be further footnoted.)

4) Harris, op. cit., 128.

5) Kensett Papers, op. cit., Edmonds to Kensett, Feb. 10, 1841.

today of the propensity of the artists in Rome lauding
Raphael and his followers to the skies and condemning
Michael Angelo. Sorry to hear an American artist say
'Damn Michael Angelo, his style was false...'" Nevertheless, the influences of both Raphael and Michelangelo can
be seen in Edmonds' monumental painting Felix Trembled,
soon to be exhibited at the Cathedral Church of St. John
the Divine in New York City, is from a private collection.

From the very beginning, Edmonds was attracted to the
Dutch masters whose paintings were probably first seen by
him in engravings. The February 10th letter to Kensett
included a request from Edmonds for any prints by Teniers,
Ostade, Wouvermans, etc., "You know I am partial to interiors." A few days later he was able to see the great
collection of Cardinal Teschi, reputed to have specimens
of the finest Dutch masters in Europe. His comment were,
"Style of painting by the Dutch school-beautiful touch-
transparent shadows-luminous effects-very little positive
colors-but when used, of the greatest value-seem first
painted up with great care and softened down so that when
the last touches were applied they told exceedingly well."
That Edmonds learned this lesson well can be seen in his
work, Reading the Scriptures, now in private hands in New
York.

Edmonds' preoccupation with color made him dislike
the work of the neo-classicists who emphasized drawing at
the expense of color. Thus, on a visit to the studio of

Baron Vincenzo Camuccini, a follower of Mengs, reputed to
be the "most distinguished Italian painter now living,"
Edmonds liked the cartoons and drawing, but criticized the
color for being too much in the "French style" and too much
like David. There was a similar reaction to Francesco
Podesti, then at work on a large painting of The Judgment
of Solomon. After many visits to galleries to view the
contemporary Italian painters, Edmonds felt that American
artists had nothing to fear. This was a common reaction
among Americans who were stupefied by the ineptitude of
the contemporary Italian artist.[6]   Edmonds amplified this
to apply to all of Europe. "...with a very few exceptions
I think they are far behind the old masters and equal to
many works by American artists who have never been abroad.
Indeed with the opportunity afforded them...I am surprised
at their deficiency."[7]

Kensett reported that on Edmonds first visit to Paris,
Edmonds was delighted with Metsu and all the Dutch school
and the coloring of Rubens, but could not respond to Titian.
Even this early, Edmonds found few in the Italian school to
like and of the Spanish school preferred Murillo.[8]   It was
not until Edmonds reached Venice that he saw pictures from
the Renaissance that pleased him. His greatest praise went

6) Harris, op. cit., 296.

7) Edmonds, "Autobiography," III, 13.

8) Kensett, "Diary," op. cit., Jan. 14, 1841.

to three pictures, Tintoretto's <u>Miracle of the Slave</u>,
Titian's <u>Presentation of the Young Virgin</u> and <u>Christ at</u>
<u>the House of Simon the Pharisee</u> by Veronese. Here, he
praised Titian, calling his work a "singular picture."
He added, "Paul Veronese can only be seen to advantage at
Venice-here his colouring is glowing and fresh-far surpass-
ing anything I have seen of his works in the Louvre-Titian's
"Assumption" is also a fine work-the Virgin...Cherubs and
Angels...very fine...rather too much red."

Edmonds must have been well acquainted with Dunlap's
<u>History</u>, published in 1834. The books reported in detail
the feelings of American artists who had been abroad and
their opinions on the great art they had seen. Gilbert
Stuart spoke somewhat slightingly of Titian's colors, but
Washington Allston was overcome by the sensations of
pleasure derived from the pictures of Titian, Tintoretto
and Veronese.[9] It is no surprise that Edmonds was pleased
by them too, because color was so important to him, but he
modified his opinions sufficiently to establish that they
were his own and not other opinions that had been watered
down.

At the end of Edmonds' first book, one of the pages
had these specific notes on Dutch painters, possibly the
result of seeing the Cardinal Teschi collection. Since

---

9) William Dunlap, <u>History of the Rise and Progress</u>
<u>of the Arts of Design in the United States</u> (2 vols. bound
as 3, New York, 1969), I, 217; II, Part 1, 162-3.

his spelling is often erratic, this is an exact reproduction:

Peter Naefs-style-architecture fine-figures
small & equisite-perspective exact-Interior
Cathedral-1 inch square
Lingelbach-Like Wouvermans-Dutch & good
Mignon-Dutch-fruit exquisite, (pealed lemon)
Jean Miel-dutch-Bingham style-good
Jean Steen-highly wrought-figures
Rachel Ruysch-famous fruit-fly on a peach
Metzer-a favorite of mine-rather wooden-
but warmly colored-& highly finished-
hands beautiful
Van der Neuf-fine figures
Francisco Van Mieris-highly finished
figures-but hard
Cornelius Bega-figures-Dutch-but hard-
Draperty highly wrought

The reference to Bingham indicates an early recognition of that man's talents. It also shows who came first in Edmonds' mind. On the occasion of viewing the Teschi collection, Edmonds wrote that he had seen two or three admirable Teniers, one beautiful Metzu (sic), besides excellent examples of Wouvermans and Ostade.

The results of this trip, with the opportunities afforded to see artists like these, can be seen in The Image Pedlar (Figure 7), at the New York Historical Society. The background of this picture is remarkably like the background in Jan Steen's The World Upside Down. Reading the Scriptures was painted in the late 1850s and is another example of the successful application of the ideas gained abroad. This picture was called worthy of a Dutch master by Barbara Novak.[10]

---

10) Barbara Novak to Author, May 1969.

Of all the Dutch painters, Edmonds admired Metsu the
most for his use of color and took a whole page in his
journal on April 20th to detail how he thought this had
been achieved. His admiration in no way prevented him from
observing that Metsu was rather wooden in his drawing.
Upon completing his color analysis, Edmonds added, "...upon
the while I think Stewart Newton had Metzu in view in form-
ing his style-Metzu is unlike Teniers, Ostand (sic), Wouvermans, or any other Dutch master I have seen." The interest
in Newton may have been sparked by the comparison drawn by
the critic of the N.Y. Mirror when Edmonds' Dominie Sampson
recalled the work of Newton to the critic. Gilbert Stuart
Newton, 1794-1835, an historical and portrait painter was
a newphew of Gilbert Stuart. His success in those fields
and in literary subjects had been very great until he went
insane and died at the age of 40.

The spring exhibit of 1841 of the Salon paintings at
the Louvre were seen by Edmonds on his return to Paris in
May. He said, "...some 2000 in number, embracing all kinds,
viz Historic, landscape, portrait, etc, etc, some very good,
some indifferent & nearly all decidedly French in execution." The best of the lot, in his estimation had been
done by Pierre Wickenberg, a Dutch artist. He described
it as, "...a Winter scene...the ice, broken and scattered,
the hovel near the shore, the sled with children wrapped

in their winter apparel, all very fine."[11] A painting by
Gué was described as "full of sublimity and poetry."[12]
Others by Delacroix were called "very good."[13] He liked
the Swiss landscapes of Calame and Coignet and a small
Dutch picture of a female and a still life by Béranger.[14]
He included three French historical pictures by Jean Alaux
for praise and concluded his remarks on the exhibition with
criticism of the American artists in the show. "Of the
American artists those of Vanderlyn and Healy are the most
prominent-but neither doing much credit to their country:
the former (a view of the falls of Niagara decidedly bad)."
George P.A. Healy had submitted five portraits. Richardson
says that Healy had extraordinary success as a portrait
painter, but that on the whole his work was uneven with
the bulk of his work dry and tiresome.[15]

The comment by Edmonds that all the paintings were
decidedly _French_ in execution was not a compliment. He
repeated it with variations throughout his journal and it
mirrored a common complaint from Americans. Thomas Cole

---

11) Musee Royal, _Explication des Ouvrages de Peinture,
Sculpture, Architecture, Graveure et Lithographie des
Artistes Vivants_ (Paris, Mar. 15, 1841), Cat. #2015,
Effet d'hiver.

12) _Ibid._, Cat. #928, Le jugement dernier.

13) _Ibid._, Cat. #310, _Un naufrage_; Cat. #311, _Noce
juive dans le Maroc_; Cat. #509, _Prise de Constantinople
par les Croises-1204._

14) _Ibid._, Cat. #120, _La Cuisiniere._

summed it up in 1831, in some notes on the Louvre exhibition of that year:

> In the first place, subjects which French
> artists seem to delight in are either
> bloody or voluptucus, death, murder,
> battle, Venuse, Psyches, are portrayed in
> a cold, hard and often tawdry style of
> color and with an almost universal de-
> ficiency in chiaroscuro. The whole arti-
> ficial and theatrical. In portrait they
> are wretched, and in landscape, cold,
> labored and artificial. (Ary) Scheffer's
> paintings are an exception and the only
> one to the previous inanimadversion. He
> has some real feeling.[16]

Durand expressed contradictory opinions that ranged from, "David appears to have sown the first seeds of a corrupt style, for, previous to his time, it appears to me that the French possessed much of the purity and chasteness of the Italian school" to "...the French artists are far superior to the English. It is true that these figures are too often academic and what is termed theatrical ...but their finished drawing, anatomical correctness, character and grandeur of composition, entitle them to an elevated rank as a school of art..."[17]

Edmonds did concur in part with the opinions of Durand and Cole, yet, when we consider the choice of art that he singled out from the 1841 Salon show, it can be seen that he selected individual pictures on their merits alone. The selections include a little bit of everything. The loose,

---

16) Parker E. Lesley, "Thomas Cole and the Romantic Sensibility," Art Quarterly, III (Fall, 1942), 211.

17) Durand, op. cit., 155.

painterly style of Delacroix and his subject matter did
not deter Edmonds from recognizing the superiority of the
artist. This was so, even though, as will be shown, Edmonds preferred the tight highly finished method he was
used to.

The exhibition, moreover, sparked ideas for paintings.
In the back of his second volume of the journal, Edmonds
made a list headed, "Subjects for Pictures on Seeing Exhibition of Modern Pictures in Paris May 1841."[18] We know
that he used some of these ideas in paintings in the years
to follow. The notes imply that there should have been at
least two sketches accompanying this list, but only one
remains. In some cases, we know that he made drawings from
these ideas, even if they were not developed further. We
may never know how many ideas he actually developed, since
not all of his paintings have descriptions, even where
there are titles.

Edmonds must have considered English painting, past
and present, as the most important, because on his return
to England he indulged in a virtual orgy of criticism.
This is as should be expected for the English influence
was still very strong in the American art world. The influence of Benjamin West through his generosity to visiting
American artists has been well documented. Any art instruction books had to come from England because none were

---

18) To be discussed in context.

printed in the United States in the early nineteenth century.
English literature too, had its greatest impact in the States
and provided ideas for many paintings by a number of artists.
As has been seen, Edmonds' attitude towards Sir Walter Scott
was positively reverential.

On his very first day in London, Edmonds went to view
the Royal Academy exhibition, consisting of some 1350 works
of art in painting, sculpture and engraving. Of these he
mentioned about two dozen specifically. He thought the
two portraits by Wilkie were only ordinary, but Cunningham has explained that Wilkie had great but unequal powers
as a portrait painter.[19] Three paintings by C.R. Leslie,
Le Bourgeois Gentilhomme, Fairlop Fair and The library at
Holland House with portraits, evoked a horrified protest,
"...oh how he has fallen off! What vile daubs these were-
crude, coarse, raw and ill defined. They seem works of an
artist not yet out of his studies." The violent reaction
to Turner was, "...truly he has run mad!" Stanfield was
seen as having done himself justice, but Danby, Allan and
Briggs were all disappointing. Although John Martin had
entered five landscapes, Pandemonium and the Celestial City,
only the last was thought worthy of him. Chalon was,
"...truly a mantuamakers favorite-ribbons, laces and tinsel
work." Cooper was commended only for his dogs and horses;
Collins was picturesque and effective, but too sketchy and

---

19) Allan Cunningham, The Life of Sir David Wilkie
(3 vols., London, 1843), III, 512.

Etty's performance indifferent in everything but the naked figure.

O Jerusalem, Jerusalem by Sir Charles Eastlake reminded Edmonds of the old masters, but he failed to say why. Henry Howard had two portraits and three story-telling pictures that found favor as well as John Prescott did with a similar assortment. Frederick Lee, the landscape painter, was favored, but Edmonds added, "...if he was not so careless would paint a picture that would last." This reflected a deep concern, often expressed, about the possible impermanence of art.

William Mulready's painting admonished, "Train up a child in the way he should go, and when he is old he will not depart from it."[20] The moralizing text struck Edmonds as "...too snuffy to please," and while he thought Mulready drew well enough, he called him a mannerist. Maclise was seen as having bestowed great labor upon some works, but, "...his subjects are badly chosen and his pictures have no tone-they look raw and chalky." In portraiture, Edmonds liked Pickersgill, but to his great surprise Sir Martin A. Shee, the president of the Royal Academy was thought by Edmonds to be the best portrait painter of all.

Thomas Webster had entered three pictures, simply titled schoolboy scenes, that Edmonds thought were very

20) Algernon Graves, Royal Academy of Arts (8 vols., London, 1905), V, 324.

clever. Perhaps, they provided some impetus for the schoolboy scenes Edmonds was to paint.

Edmonds and Durand agreed in 1841 that they did not
care for Turner.[21] It is not surprising that they should
agree given their common backgrounds in art and engraving.
The kind of esthetic in art that they agreed on was aptly
expressed by Daniel Huntington in his Memorial Address on
Durand:

> He (Durand) maintained that a landscape-
> painter in his early studies should not
> only make careful copies of nature in the
> fields, but be trained by drawing the human
> figure, both from the antique and the liv-
> ing model. Accuracy of eye, with facility
> and exactness, can rarely, if ever, be ac-
> quired without such practice...The forms
> of inanimate nature seldom demand absolute
> accuracy of drawing; but in accessory
> figures, buildings and animals, it is es-
> sential. Durand...was habitually true and
> exact; yet he dwelt with great fondness
> on those qualities which depend on the
> processes and mysteries of the art...[22]

After seeing many more of Turner's works, Edmonds expanded his ideas in journal on July 11th. He found much
to admire in Turner's first style and thought it well
worthy of close study. He said that Turner had, "...kept
nature in view and yet followed Claude sufficiently to
paint some of the finest landscapes I ever saw." Edmonds
confessed that he found himself among the group that could
not stand Turner's current style at all, although there

---

21) Durand, op. cit., 150.

22) Ibid., 209-10.

were many who admired it greatly. His reason was that,
"I believe his present style is pernicious to the younger
artists who are too fond of imitating him." A description of Turner's style as seen by Edmonds follows:

> Suppose a piece of canvas 3 feet by $3\frac{1}{2}$
> feet covered with paint skins and paint
> as indiscriminately as the side of a com-
> mon house painters walls where he cleans
> his bushes, without a single object de-
> fined so as to enable you to distinguish
> a tree from a camel leopard, excepting
> immediately in the foreground where there
> is a snake about two inches long clearly
> and distinctly drawn, and you have a finished
> picture by Turner-In other words one might
> cut a little snake out of a childs primer
> book and lay it upon the floor where there
> are a map of colors reflected from a prism
> and call it a picture with as much truth
> as he could call Mr. Turner's landscape-
> It is perhaps a picture literally speak-
> ing; but it is a picture without design,
> without composition, without drawing and
> without anything else that makes painting
> an intellectual art.

Although Durand was to modify his opinion of Turner
in later years, on this visit he was unable to discern that
high degree of excellence conceded to him. "He appears to
me, indeed, the most factitious and artificial of all the
distinguished English artists. I discover in him much of
imaginative and poetic power, but that appears developed
at too great a sacrifice of truth and propriety...if
Turner is to be judged by the acknowledged standard of
excellence presented in the works of the Old Masters, or
by nature in the commonly received acceptance of the term,

he must be found wanting."[23]

Durand had a poor opinion of the English school in general, but made notable exceptions of Landseer and Constable. He thought their English manner too artificial and without the spiritual or intellectual meaning so essential to art. Like Edmonds, he did not care for the late works of Leslie or Wilkie because they had turned, "...from their former chaste and true style to the present superficial or negligent, or rather studiously careless, manner of their contemporaries."[24]

C.R. Leslie was one of the contemporary artists upon whom Edmonds decided to expand his earlier remarks. Edmonds felt that Leslie fell from his estate because of his attempts to imitate Turner, that he was never a good colorist and that he had forsaken his great talents as a designer. Edmonds had gone on, "He too thinks all light is white and all warm colors must be purple or india red."

The ensuing remarks by Edmonds, reflect, perhaps, the disparity between engravings viewed in America with the reality of the paintings they were based on as seen abroad. "...the English engravers spoil such men as Turner & Leslie—For they are so artist-like in their way, that one of Leslie's present daubs looks equally well when engraved as one of his most highly finished works—The truth is the

23) Durand, op. cit., 150-1.
24) Ibid., 152-3.

engraver finishes what the painter leaves undone and this
makes the painter careless in execution."

Wilkie was the object of great admiration from Edmonds, particularly in his earlier works, so that Edmonds
devoted two lengthy paragraphs on the same day to his
ideas. According to Edmonds, Wilkie was one of the few
English artists to be appreciated on the continent where
the English school, in general, was not highly spoken of.
The difference, as Edmonds saw it, was that "The French,
Italian and other European artists look more to the effect
the picture is to have upon the mind than upon the eye of
the spectator. While the English are contented with at-
tracting attention by strong effects, brilliant coloring
and a fascinating tone. Wilkie was one who combined both
of these qualities in his works." Edmonds chose The
Village Festival as the best of Wilkie and "one of the
most perfect of the kind ever executed." Not only did it
have the care and finish of the Dutch, but in design, color,
effect and expression equalled any in Europe. Edmonds did
feel, however, that the quantity of paint laid upon the
canvas by Wilkie appeared too thin to be permanent. Again,
he is concerned about the permanence of painting.

Edmonds forgave Wilkie for falling off in his later
days because, "...this was from necessity: he had a complaint in his head that forbid too close application."
Perhaps, Edmonds identified with Wilkie in this matter because, since his own breakdown, he, too, suffered from

headaches.

Edmonds did not care for Wilkie's full length portraits that he had seen in various places. With the exception of the portrait of the Duke of Sussex in Buckingham Palace, Edmonds felt that Wilkie was not as happy with them as with his smaller works. Durand agreed with Edmonds, when, on his first visit to London in June 1840, he was able to visit Wilkie. Wilkie had a picture in progress of Columbus with figures as large as life, but a picture that Durand thought of inferior merit as compared with his smaller works.[25]

When Cunningham discussed the great epochs in the work of Wilkie, he justified the second style by saying that Wilkie had not lived to work out this style, but, in the meantime, the public complained of the change as an insult as well as an injury.[26] As we have seen, Edmonds found another way to justify the change, although he had to be aware of these other opinions.

Sandby described the paintings of Daniel Maclise thus: "Most of his works are of large size, crowded with figures and elaborately finished in all the accessories and details. He is a gorgeous colorist...choice of subjects and the mode of treating them indicate his

---

25) Durand, op. cit., 149.

26) Cunningham, op. cit., III, 494-5.

originality."[27] Edmonds agreed that Maclise was:

> ...an artist that draws elaborately and
> correctly and shows great research and
> study as an artist and yet the Brick dust
> so pervades his works that it makes one's
> eyes sore to look at them-his shadows, re-
> flections and everything else is red and
> white: and the worst kind of red to be
> left raw upon the canvas-to wit-a sort
> of purple red-his lights too are all
> white wash, totally devoid of anything
> warm, mellow or transparent.

Edmonds was human enough to let his warm personal opinion

of a man color his feelings about him as an artist as he

did with Clarkson Stanfield. Edmonds forgave the opacity

in Stanfield's paintings because he was once a scene

painter. He praised Stanfield's accurate drawing and

"...finishes with great care and still preserves all the

freedom one likes to see in an artists handling-some

critics think he allows the drab colors to pervade his

his works...I saw nothing in the...present exhibition

that would admit of that charge...a very communicate,

agreeable companion." Sandby implied that Stanfield was

always something of a scene painter instead of an artist

because he was never able to achieve gradations of

atmosphere.[28]

Edmonds was very favorably impressed by the portraits

done by Sir Henry Raeburn:

> I could not but be pleased with the bold
> shadows and great breadth of light so

---

27) William Sandby, The History of the Royal Academy
of Arts (2 vols., London, 1862), II, 162.

28) Ibid., II, 151-2.

>visible in his works. Those who have seen
>his portrait of Dugald Stewart in the
>Philadelphia Academy of Fine Arts will
>have a good idea of his style. His full
>length portrait of Sir Walter Scott at
>Abbotsford I did not like as well-his shadows
>were rather opaque and the dress and back-
>ground wanted a little more detail.

Sandby described Raeburn's style as free and bold, his draw-

ing extremely correct, his coloring, rich, deep and har-

monious.[29] Cunningham not only praised Raeburn, but es-

pecially the portrait of Sir Walter Scott that Edmonds dis-

liked.[30] Dunlap mentioned that Raeburn had been elected an

honorary member to the Academy of Fine Arts in New York and

South Carolina, so that his work was well known and must

have been thoroughly discussed in America.[31] Edmonds had

his own ideas.

Cunningham praised Sir Thomas Lawrence extravagantly

for his, "...natural splendour of coloring...like sunshine

in dew, is as refreshing as lustrous...he saw but living

life: his genius was for the court, the elegance of fashion

and the bloom of the hour."[32] Sandby, less laudatory, still

said, "...if his pictures seldom possess the mellow sweetness

of Reynolds he as often surpassed him in some...qualities."[33]

---

29) Sandby, I, 351.

30) Allan Cunningham, The Lives of the Most Eminent
British Painters and Sculptors (6 vols., New York, 1832),
V, 225.

31) Dunlap, History, op. cit., I, 426.

32) Cunningham, op. cit., VI, 269.

33) Sandby, op. cit., II, 32.

Dunlap's History carried Malbone's estimation of Lawrence
as "the best portrait painter."[34] Edmonds selected
Lawrence's portrait of Benjamin West, but, in general
was disappointed. The pictures were:

> ...too painty-and wanted the warm mellow
> tone of Sir Joshua Reynolds. He glazed
> very little; painted in and apparently
> finished in a few sittings and seemed to
> care for little else than the air of
> gentility which a velvet color and a well
> tied cravat, for which his portraits are
> so famous. His shadows and middle tints
> were generally made of umber, so that his
> portraits when done more nearly resemble
> a delicate India Ink drawing, slightly
> touched in with a little color. His
> drapery was hard and tinny and wanted the
> looseness so famous in Sir Joshua's
> drapery.

When Edmonds visited the British Institute on July
6th, he saw the works of deceased British artists, "...to
wit-Reynolds, Gainsborough, Wilson, Hogarth, Newton and
Stoddarth-and on this account valuable to me." Edmonds
dwelt in detail on the manner of Reynold's painting which
he admired, but was distressed that some of them had faded
in color. He singled out Reynold's portrait of Sterne and
several others as fine specimens:

> Sterne is in excellent preservation and
> full of expression and character-several
> ...lady portraits exhibit all the grace
> and liveliness for which he was so cele-
> brated...must have placed his sitters on
> a platform and so arranged them as to have
> as little shadow on the face as possible...
> avoided too in a masterly manner the old
> trick of keeping the lower part of the face

---

34) Dunlap, History, op. cit., II, 18.

> down so low as to make the lights upon
> the forehead tell with unnatural force.
> This is difficult, but it is true to life
> and when well done gives great breadth to
> the countenance. In his female portraits
> his shadows under the nose eyebrows are
> very light and scarcely perceptible. His
> greys are pearly and delicate and no brick
> dust visible in any part. Indeed Red
> seems to be discarded from his pallette
> except in the lips, on the cheeks and
> round the corner of the eyes, and in these
> spots it is vermilion mixed with white.

According to Thornbury, Reynolds worked standing, so that he could perpetually recede and advance to his sitter.[35] It is also possible that he placed his sitters on a platform as Edmonds thought. Thornbury described how Reynolds used red. "When Sir Joshua was using fleeting lake and carmines for his flesh and trying to retain the fugitive colors by imprisoning them in imperishable cages of varnish, he used to get very petulant, if anyone told him vermilion was more durable."[36] A good Reynolds was described as having, "...the old Stilton texture, the tone of a picture 'boiled in brandy,' the mellow yellows, the transparent reds, the sunny browns...We may regret his pictures have faded...cannot reproach (him)...for making experiments in coloring..."[37]

Edmonds' remarks on Gainsborough were very brief because he did not care for his landscapes except in tone. He thought they were too sketchy and mannered and "...seem

---

35) Walter Thornbury, British Artists from Hogarth to Turner (2 vols., London, 1861), I, 269.

36) Thornbury, op. cit., I, 215.

37) Ibid., I, 220-1.

mostly to be made out with Hatchings in asphaltum." Sir
Joshua had also sneered at Gainsborough's manner, yet he
had had to confess that, "...all those odd scratches and
marks...by a kind of magic, at a certain distance, assumed
forms and dropped into their places."[38]

Wilson's landscapes were more pleasing to Edmonds who
thought that some were quite, "Claude like and poetical in
composition," but that Wilson was too much of a mannerist
with a touch that looked like worm tracks. Sandby implied
that Wilson was somewhat less than original, although,
"...in choice of subject, felicity in the distribution of
light and shade, freshness and harmony of tints he was
scarcely excelled."[39] Cunningham praised Wilson for noble
conceptions, vigorous execution and harmonious arrangements.[40]

Edmonds did not respond enthusiastically to Hogarth
as might have been expected from their common interest in
genre. He saw Hogarth as the same in all his works,
"...aiming at expression and character and indifferent of
execution—Still Hogarth paints some things capitally well."
This, despite Leslie's opinion, repeated by Dunlap on
"Hogarth's matchless pictures."[41]

---

38) Thornbury, op. cit., I, 23.

39) Sandby, op. cit., I, 109.

40) Cunningham, Lives, op. cit., II, 210.

41) Dunlap, History, op. cit., I, 55.

Edmonds approved of Gilbert Stuart Newton because he
was "a sweet colorist." Edmonds said that his:

> ...feeling for color is natural and he
> seems to have loved his brush and played
> with it, with as much fondness as a lover
> would with his mistress. Everything on
> Newton's canvas is made of tints-if he
> paints a bit of yellow drapery even if it
> be but a petticoat, still it contains when
> closely examined red, blue, green, grey
> and purple & yet as a whole it is in per-
> fect keeping...

Sandby agreed, "...fine natural perception of color, intro-
ducing innumerable gradations, in which respect his pictures
rank among the best in the English school."[42] Leslie said
that Newton was blessed with an exquisite eye for color.[43]
No wonder Edmonds was pleased to be linked with Newton.

The last established artist considered by Edmonds was
Thomas Stothard, whose work did not impress Edmonds. He
said, "...perhaps his compositions are poetical and all that
sort of thing, but he is too frequently stiff and formal
and paints without a good feeling for color." Turner had
admired Stothard, naming him the "Giotto of England," but
Sandby felt that Stothard's oil paintings were deficient in
color and wanting in force and too much like water colors.[44]

E.P. Richardson has maintained that the second genera-
tion of romanticists, 1825-1850, exhibited a striking

---

42) Sandby, op. cit., II, 149.

43) Dunlap, History, op. cit., II, 301.

44) Sandby, op. cit., I, 303.

absence of esthetic dogma and a relative weakness of literary influences. Yet, Flexner says, "At no other time has
our painting been, for better or worse, so original, so
far from European attitudes and forms."[45] Flexner explained how, after the War of 1812, America had been removed from transatlantic turmoils. "Europe was wallowing
in wars, tyrannies, and abortive revolutions that were
fostering in art pessimism, violence, revolt, despair: a
cold classicism or emphasis on those aspects of romantic
thinking that denied ordinary experience...While the most-
admired schools abroad were eschewing ordinary life, the
Native School began its concentration on local landscape
and genre."[46]

There has been very little direct information on the
kind of art material that was used for instruction in those
early days. The influence of England remained strong in
the arts and literature, if for no other reason than the
common language. A volume of essays has been indirectly
brought to light by notations in Edmonds' travel journal.
After viewing a number of paintings, he noted, next to
several, that they were "in Burnet." Further research
brought to light A Treatise on Paintings by John Burnet.[47]

---

45) James T. Flexner, That Wilder Image (New York,
1962), xii.

46) Flexner, op. cit., xii.

47) John Burnet, A Treatise on Painting in Four Parts
(London, 1850).

Each of the essays had been published separately, the first
in 1822, the second in 1826, the third in 1827, but the
last not until 1837.

Each essay deals with a different problem confronted
by artists, but the overriding emphasis is that for each
problem the artist must go to nature to observe. The first
essay, Practical Hints on Composition in Painting, had sub-
headings on Angular and Circular Composition. The first
advice was that "Concealing the art is one of its greatest
beauties..."[48] Plates were provided, engraved by John ·
Burnet, illustrating old and modern masters in order to
demonstrate compositional points. Burnet concluded this
essay with advice:

> I must also caution the young artist
> against supposing that these modes of
> arrangement are given for his imitation
> ...One great cause of obscurity which en-
> velopes the art is the criticism of those
> whose ideas on the subject are obscure,-
> to free the world from this influence is
> perhaps impossible; but the artist must
> free himself.[49]

The second essay, Practical Hints on Light and Shade
in Painting, consisted of illustrations with the discussion
relating to each one. Here, examples from the Dutch school
predominated. In one figure by Rembrandt of a woman holding
a baby, Burnet called attention to how small a portion of
light could engage Rembrandt's solicitude.[50] Both interiors

48) Burnet, Composition, op. cit., 9.

49) Ibid., 31.

50) Ibid., Light and Shade, op. cit., 15.

and exteriors were discussed.

The third essay, <u>Practical Hints on Colour in Painting</u>, had hand-colored plates, of necessity, in water color. The colors of the iris and how it added up to 100 was explained, as were color values. Warm and cold colors were differentiated and the differences that light had upon color when seen outdoors was explained. Titian was highly praised, but "...In comparing Titian with Veronese... general warmth diffused over works of the former...The Veronese possess the freshness of morn when the dewy moisture spreads a delicate veil over the scene...We seek in vain in...Titian for those delicate gray tones...in the flesh of Venus."[51] Reynolds was cited frequently from the <u>Discourses</u>. But all the essays return again and again to nature as the final arbiter.

Nationalism, combined with the American feeling about the uniqueness of their surroundings, fitted in with this call to turn to nature. The American esthetic in landscape was reflected in the delight in the wildness of the landscape. Their love of nature was the city man's nostalgia combined with cultural nationalism, but they also feared their delight in nature because it might be only a sensuous experience that could sap moral fiber.[52]

---

51) Burnet, <u>Colour</u>, <u>op. cit.</u>, 30.

52) Frankenstein, Lecture, <u>op. cit.</u>, June 24, 1970.

An example of the trend of thought among Americans can
be seen in the introduction to the NAD catalogue of 1837.
It said that painting, "...leads the mind to contemplation
of the infinite and varied beauties of creation and directs
the thoughs of Nature up to Nature's God."

Durand called for imagination and poetic power. The
means to implement this was to come from accuracy of eye
with facility and exactness in drawing. His standard of excellence was derived from the old masters or by nature in
the common acceptance of the term. Durand did not care for
most of the English school, because he thought their manner
too artificial and without the spiritual or intellectual
meaning so essential to art.[53]

Nationalism was one of the factors that promoted American fascination with genre. Patriots wished to think of
their fellow nationals as a unique order of man. The growth
of Jacksonian democracy and its association with the American belief in its manifest destiny was another factor.

Thus the exhortations from Burnet to look towards nature fell upon fertile ground. Mount was one of the first
to state the ideal of the Native School that most separated
it from European practice. A picture should seem less the
work of a human hand than an actual slice of nature.[54] Edmonds summed up his ideal of what a painting should be when

---

53) Durand, op. cit., 150-3.

54) Flexner, op. cit., 34.

he described what he thought Wilkie had achieved. Wilkie
combined the effect a picture had upon the mind of the
spectator with strong effects, brilliant coloring and a
fascinating tone.

For Americans, the effect upon the mind was where the
crucial difference occurred that broke with the European
school. In this period, when the pantheistic philosophies
of Emerson were being widely accepted, the American artist
responded with efforts to illustrate these philosophies.
Along with a pantheistic reverence for inanimate nature
went optimism and a morality that avoided churches. Durand
felt that the artist's concern was not self-expression but
reverent interpretation, so that a viewer would feel that
he was not looking at a picture but at nature's own face.[55]

In order to achieve their esthetic, their style broke
with the Europeans in its emphasis on nature, suppression
of the subjective hand of the artist and the difference
in the treatment of tonality and light.

The esthetic of the American artist did not hold that
the ideal must be opposed to the real, but rather that the
perfection of the real must be sought as an uplifting experience for the artist and the viewer. This should not
and did not lead to the neoclassical but to the American
ideal of how nature in landscape, genre, portrait or any
subject should be presented.

---

55) Flexner, op. cit., 73.

The reactions and the paintings of Durand and Edmonds can be cited as an example of the American esthetic. The notations in Edmonds' journal and the kind of painting that was produced up to 1840 supports the assumption that the first three essays by Burnet were studied in the early day of the NAD and fed the esthetic that the Americans developed.

The alleged weakness of literary influence does not hold up, either. Some of the difficulty on this point may lie in the fact that titles of paintings were not always readily identifiable as stemming from a literary source. Edmonds' paintings and their titles are notable examples. But many artists experimented with literary topics.

The fourth essay by Burnet, Education of the Eye, was not published until 1837, so does not contribute to the idea that an esthetic had been formed by that time. A survey of the painting of the period, along with the perusal of the Burnet essays, strengthens the belief that these essays were used and contributed to the formation of the American esthetic.

CHAPTER IV

Productive Years, 1842-1852

"As I had much to do in my business towards bringing up 'back work' and as my head was still 'ailing' I did not commence a picture until the following winter when I painted the Bashful Cousin for my friend Jonathan Sturges."[1] This was Edmonds' explanation of his return to the workaday world in New York, but he neglected an interesting piece of information. On Nov. 4, 1841, he had been married to Dorothea Lord.[2] His total bereavement had lasted less than a year, but there were two young children to be cared for. This marriage, apparently happy, resulted in six more children.[3]

From this time until 1855, Edmonds' business career ran smoothly and prosperously. In 1842, there was the first indication in Edmonds' story that a successful banker could be, and frequently was, involved in politics. Using Mechanics' Bank stationery, Edmonds wrote to State Comptroller A.C. Flagg about a loan that the bank made to the

---

1) Edmonds, "Autobiography, III, 5.

2) Jean Mackinnon Holt, "Francis William Edmonds," in Allen Johnson ed., Dictionary of American Biography (11 vols., New York, 1927-58), III, 22. (Hereafter DAB).

3) Cummings, op. cit., 319.

State of New York, but had been only partially repaid.[4]
Edmonds' had mentioned briefly in his autobiography that
in 1843 he had been absent from the city.[5] A letter to
W.C. Bryant, headed "Albany, Jan. 27, 1843," had the clue
to his whereabouts and the reason for his absence. The
letter thanked Bryant for one received by Edmonds the previous day that was laudatory of Edmonds. Edmonds said, in
part, "No one could have endeavored to discharge the duties
of life more honestly and truly than I have; and having
resisted evil when surrounded by temptation, I am extremely
sensitive to the wholesale abuse that is poured (somewhat
justly I admit) upon the head, of all those who have been
so unfortunate as to have their destinies cast in the same
mould with 'Monied Corporations.'"[6]

Edmonds continued in this fashion, becoming almost
maudlin in the expression of his emotions. The last
sentence, however, would be extremely important when viewed
in the light of later difficulties. "As I have been most
sorely rebuked since I have been in this city for uniting
in my person that strange compound a Bank officer and a
Democrat."[7] Edmonds undoubtedly became a Democrat through

---

4) A.C. Flagg Papers, Mss. Division, New York Public
Library, Edmonds to Flagg, Feb. 15, 1842.

5) Edmonds, "Autobiography," III, 16.

6) W.C. Bryant Papers (New York Public Library, Mss.
Division), F.W. Edmonds to W.C. Bryant, Jan. 27, 1843.

7) Ibid.

the influence of his brother, John Worth Edmonds, who started his law career as a clerk in Martin Van Buren's office.[8] John Worth Edmonds has been described as, "...a rising young Democratic politician of radical leanings, in the confidence of the Regency..."[9] He has been credited with winning union labor's first victory in the United States.[10]

The state legislature was sitting in Albany in January 1843 and there were at least two bills under consideration that would account for Edmonds' presence there, probably as a lobbyist. A bill was up to reduce the capital stock of the Mechanics' Bank of New York City.[11] Comptroller Flagg's report to the legislature, reported at length in the N.Y. Evening Post, dealt with the problem of railroad organization and financing.[12] That this second matter concerned Edmonds is confirmed by a letter to Flagg, dated Oct. 9, 1843. A clipping was enclosed that gave the names of the 12 new directors of the New York and Erie Railroad, among them was F.W. Edmonds. The letter, an expression of

---

8) Lucien Brock, The Bench and Bar of New York (2 vols., New York, 1870), I, 317.

9) Arthur M. Schlesinger, Jr., The Age of Jackson (New York, 1946), 197.

10) Ibid., 198, fn. 23.

11) New York Evening Post, Jan. 20, 1843.

12) Ibid., Jan. 27, 1843.

independence, said:

> The new directors from this city are
> thorough business men and will not be
> the instrument of any party heretofore
> connected with the road. I don't know
> that one of them owns a dollar of stock
> or has any direct personal interest in
> it. They come in looking to individual
> enterprise alone for aid-and if this is
> to be denied they will leave it with a
> promptness that will show to the public
> they are not men to be buried beneath
> the falling ruins of a rotten concern
> or to be humbug'd with the visionary
> projects of restless speculators. [13]

Sometime in the 40s, Edmonds became a director of the

Harlem Railroad and by 1850 was listed as a director in the

Broadway Insurance Co.[14] Although this is theoretically

too early for interlocking directorates, the principle was

the same; those in high places had the access to other

high places.

A painting by Edmonds, The Sleeping Ostler, was ex-

hibited in the October 1841 exhibition of the Apollo

Association. It was probably executed and submitted be-

fore Edmonds' illness and trip to Europe. The only informa-

tion on it is that it was purchased by Edmond's brother,

John Worth Edmonds. The presumption on The Bashful Cousin,

painted for Sturges and exhibited at the NAD in 1842 is that

it is still in existence because Larkin discussed its brush-

work.[15]

---

13) Flagg Papers, op. cit.

14) Altmann, op. cit., 72.

15) Oliver W. Larkin, Art and Life in America
(Revised ed., New York, 1966), 220.

The second picture Edmonds' showed at the NAD in 1842 was The Italian Mendicants and it was preferred by the Knickerbocker's critic:

> In this picture we discover that the artist has availed himself of his trip abroad to improve his style. Those who have traveled in Italy have noticed and been annoyed by the swarms of beggars that people that classic land, and have been struck with their apostle-like appearance as exhibited in the works of the old masters; their long beards and sun-burnt countenances. Mr. Edmonds has given us a very faithful picture of one of these characters, accompanied by his daughter. There is a brightness and clearness in the whole picture perfectly in keeping with the subject, for Italy with all her wretchedness still wears a cheerful aspect, and her mendicants, though begging with a doleful countenance at one moment, are the next dancing with light hearts and lively steps to a mountaineer's pipe. Mr. Edmonds' pictures please us for their correct composition, great breath of light and shade and judicious arrangement of color. The visitor will notice the entire dissimularity of style as exhibited in the two paintings. We observe with pleasure the great care Mr. Edmonds bestows on the detail of his pictures.[16]

Edmonds felt that although the Mendicants was an attractive exhibition picture, the Bashful Cousin was the best of the two.[17] The idea for the Italian Mendicants was one of those listed by Edmonds after he had viewed the Salon exhibition in Paris in 1841. He wrote, "Old man and his daughter (young say 12) the latter begging for

---

16) Knickerbocker, XIX (June 1842), 591.

17) Edmonds, "Autobiography," III, 16.

<u>alms</u>-half length life size."[18] An oil sketch of a head
of one of the beggars exists in a private collection in
New York that fully accords with the description of their
"apostle-like appearance" (Figure 8).

Edmonds barely mentioned his only painting for 1843,
but the <u>Knickerbocker</u> praised it in detail:

> No. 190, <u>Boy Stealing Milk</u> by Francis
> William Edmonds. Having "satisfied the
> sentiment" of this picture, by a survey
> of the threatening aspect of the old lady;
> the sort of mesmeric consciousness of her
> presence, expressed in the half-satisfied
> half-fearful countenance of her victim;
> and the evident <u>coolness</u> of the atmosphere
> in the apartment, we would counsel exami-
> nation of the correct drawing of the
> figures, and the finish and naturalness
> of the accessories. Observe the <u>tin</u> of
> the milk-pan, the dripping line of rich
> deposit left by the receding fluid, and
> the thick stream <u>debouching</u> into the young
> thief's mouth; the "hitched-up" jacket,
> the jug and <u>that</u> cabbage; and the interior
> of the upper shelves of the cupboard.
> These are so faithfully represented, that
> they form an excellent study for those
> who deem that labor lost which is devoted
> to the exhibition of truth in little
> things.[19]

Edmonds entered six paintings in the 1844 exhibition
at the NAD. Three were Italian landscapes that seem to
have been quite a departure for the genre-oriented Edmonds,
but were they? A descendant on Long Island holds a charm-
ing little Italian landscape in water color that showed
his ability. It raises a question in regard to two

---

18) Edmonds, "Travel Journal," II, back page.

19) <u>Knickerbocker</u>, XXI (June 1843), 581.

paintings that were exhibited at the NAD for sale in 1830
that were attributed to "J. Williams," although Edmonds
laid no claim to them.[20] It should be noted that the NAD
catalogue of 1838 had mistakenly attributed two of Edmonds'
pictures to "J. Williams" for which Edmonds did take the
credit.[21]

The Image Pedlar was a favorite of the critics and
Edmonds admitted that it, "...cost me a vast deal of study
and labor-It contains 9 figures besides a host of acces-
sories-all of which were painted from life-and altho pronounced by artists and men of taste to be the best picture
I ever painted was not as attractive as The Beggar's
Petition painted in the same year-This last picture is what
is termed a knee picture of the size of life and very attractive in an Exhibition because of its boldness, size
and effect."[22] The latter picture was another that came
from Edmonds' list of ideas obtained from the Paris Salon.
His idea was for "A Beggar and her child at a window
soliciting alms, the latter very young (3 or 4)."[23]

The reviewer said, "'Beggar's Petition,' is a spirited
and faithful representation of the cold indifference to
the wants of others, displayed in the miser's disposition.

---

20) Cowdrey, NAD Cat., op. cit., 210.

21) Ibid.

22) Edmonds, "Autobiography," III, 16.

23) Edmonds, "Travel Journal," II, back page.

The figures are of life-size and well drawn. The female supplicating in behalf of the distressed is graceful in attitude, and admirably contrasted with the hoarding miser."[24] The receipt of The Image Pedlar was so very much better that is surprising to find that Edmonds reacted with bitterness. "...I have become persuaded that if an artist wants to make a stir in an Exhibition he must not rely upon the merit of his work but upon its peculiar attractiveness. How far he ought to court the popular eye by resorting to such means I will not pretend to say."[25]

The Image Pedlar was described as being an effort of high order:

> ...for the artist has attempted and success-
> fully, too, to elevate the class of works to
> which it belongs. In short he has invested
> a humble subject with moral dignity, which
> we hope our younger artists who paint in
> this department will not lose sight of. An
> independent farmer has his family around him,
> apparently immediately after dinner, and a
> strolling pedler appears among them to dis-
> pose of his ware; and this gives interest to
> the whole group. The grandmother drops her
> peeling knife and the mother takes her infant
> from the cradle, to gaze at the sights in the
> pedler's basket. The husband, who has been
> reading in the cool breeze at the window, turns
> to participate in the sport, while the grand-
> father takes a bust of Washington, places it
> on the table and commences an earnest elucida-
> tion of the character of the "Father of His
> Country" to the little children around him.
> All the figures are intelligent and the whole
> scene conveys to mind a happy family. In
> color light and shade and composition, it is

24) Knickerbocker, XXIII (June 1844), 597.

25) Edmonds, "Autobiography," III, 17.

> masterly; and we see in it that minuteness
> of detail and careful finish are not incom-
> patible with a broad and luminous effort.[26]

The Image Pedlar can be seen today at the New-York
Historical Society, Accession #1858.71, where one may see
how well the critic described the painting. It is possible
that Edmonds had seen Steen's The World Upside Down, now in
Vienna at the Kunsthistorisches Museum, whose background is
so similar, and decided to turn it right side up. The ex-
plicit nature of some of the characters may reflect autobiographical memories as has been suggested with Sparking.

The Royal Academy exhibition in London in 1845 included the painting, but titled as The Image Dealer,
catalogue #656. G.P. Putnam was in the process of assembl-
ing his book, American Facts, and took pictures by Durand,
Edmonds, Ingham and Inman to England in order to have engravings taken from them.[27] The fate the pictures suffered
was reported in a magazine article. First, in reference
to Inman's portrait of Mrs. G.P. Putnam, "This work is hung
so high that it is difficult to distinguish its nicer qualities." As for the others, "...Probably they were hung so
that they could not be seen at all."[28]

---

26) Knickerbocker, XXIII (June 1844), 597.

27) Durand Papers, op. cit., G.P. Putnam to A.B.
Durand, April 3, 1845.

28) Broadway Journal, I (June 28, 1845), 403.

Putnam's book carried this laudatory paragraph:

> Edmonds is a rare impersonation of amateur
> genius in an ungenial atmosphere. He is
> one of the ablest and busiest financiers
> in busy New York, and yet he finds time to
> amuse himself, and delight others by some
> of the happiest pictures of familiar life
> which the Academy has to display. He has
> chiefly painted figure pieces and groups
> in humble life, and some of these unpre-
> tending specimens of his talent would not
> be out of place even by the side of Wilkie;
> while they yet have a character of their
> own.[29]

Sam Weller was another of the pictures in the 1844

NAD exhibit, but we have no contemporary criticism or des-

cription. The painting is described in a 1949 Parke-

Bernet catalogue as: "Depicting a youth in brown, green

and scarlet costume, with high-crowned hat, leaning

against a low wall shining a riding boot. Behind is a

balustrade and view of village houses. Signed. 30 x 24$\frac{1}{4}$."[30]

Sam Weller is a character from The Posthumous Papers of

the Pickwick Club by Dickens.[31]

On March 13, 1844, a special meeting was called at the

NAD for the specific purpose of passing a resolution support-

ing the establishment of the Permanent Gallery and for no

other purpose.[32] In May of that year, another resolution

---

29) G.P. Putnam, American Facts (London, 1845), 122.

30) Parke-Bernet Catalogue, Jan. 6-8, 1949.

31) Charles Dickens, The Posthumous Papers of the
Pickwick Club (London, n.d.), 103-4.

32) Cummings, op. cit., 178.

was passed for the formation of the "Society" that afterwards became the New-York Gallery of Fine Arts, based on
the Luman Reed collection. A number of conditions were
drawn up, with a lifetime membership set at the cost of one
dollar. Edmonds and his new father-in-law, Joseph N. Lord,
were included in the long list of trustees. The Gallery
was incorporated the following year and by 1848 the catalogue
listed Edmonds as Vice-President.[33] The same catalogue
listed The Image Pedlar among the paintings in the permanent
collection, donated by Edmonds.

The executives of the NAD at this time included Samuel
F.B. Morse, A.B. Durand and F.W. Edmonds, all of whom had
been abroad and were no doubt, impressed with the values of
the museums they had seen.[34] This incident serves to illustrate the close, almost incestuous, nature of all the artistic and cultural organizations then in existence in the City
of New York.

The Gallery had its first exhibition in the fall of
1844. Edmonds' deep involvement in and responsibilities for
the gallery emerge from a letter to Durand who was in King-
ston. Their holdings were so limited that they had to borrow
pictures from collectors and Mrs. Luman Reed contributed $500
in cash and about $500 worth of engravings as well. Edmonds

---

33) Cummings, op. cit., 178-9; New-York Gallery of
Fine Arts Catalogue 1848.

34) Cummings, op. cit., 173; Cowdrey, NAD Cat. op. cit.,
143.

hung the pictures alone, although, "I tried to avoid this responsibility-for I know I shall give cause of complaint-but there was no one else to do it-Gen'l Cummings is out of town, and he is the only artist on the Committee besides my-self."[35] The third page of the letter had sketches of the projected layout for each wall, with the titles listed below each layout.

Wall #1
    1,3,4,5,7-Cole's Course of Empire.
    2-Flagg's Girl and Child sitting down.
    6-Flagg's Match girl.
    8-Durand's Governor Stuyvesant.
    9-Mount's barn scene.
    10-Cole's Italian landscape.
    11,12,13-Sundry small pictures.
    14-Playing chess by Flagg.

Wall #2
    1-Cole's little Catskills.
    2-uncertain.
    3-Greys lady of Sturges.
    4-Cole's Sicily (Mulligan).
    5-Durand's copy of Titian.
    6-Mount's Bargaining.
    7-Moreland.
    8 & 10 Flagg's large pictures.

Wall #3
    1-Durand's pedlar.
    2-Durand's Stranded Ship.
    3-Dance on battery.
    4-Leupp's Huntington.
    5-Durand's Mrs. Washington.
    6-The dog piece.[36]

George W. Flagg studied for a while under his uncle, Washington Allston and under the patronage of Luman Reed, he studied abroad, for a time. This accounts for the pictures

---

35) Durand Papers, op. cit., Edmonds to A.B. Durand, Sept. 16, 1844.

36) Ibid.

by Flagg in the Reed collection.[37] The gallery had trouble
staying in existence from the beginning, making a number of
moves in an effort to maintain itself, but by 1850 it
opened its own quarters. The AAU Bulletin carried a paragraph on the opening:

> Mr. Ingham alluded in a few remarks to
> the obligations the friends of art were
> under to Messrs. Sturges, Leupp and Ed-
> monds for their liberality in contributing
> to the erection of the Galleries. Mr.
> Edmonds disclaimed his part of the compli-
> ment, and spoke at some length upon the
> benefit that might be rendered to the
> cause of art by liberally carrying out the
> project of which the New-York Gallery was
> the commencement.[38]

Despite all the efforts to maintain the Gallery and
all the contributions of money and paintings, by 1857 it
closed down. Some 75-100 paintings, besides sculpture and
prints, were deposited at the New-York Historical Society
where Edmonds was a member.[39] It is possible that the
difficulties that the Gallery had faced up to that time
were finally brought to a climax by the crisis of 1857,
which one authority has described as "marking a major business and commercial recession."[40]

---

37) Groce and Wallace, op. cit., 230.

38) American Art-Union Bulletin (Oct. 1850), 115.
(Hereafter AAU).

39) R.W.G. Vail, Knickerbocker Birthday (New York,
1954), 108.

40) Taylor, op. cit., 350.

During the winter of 1844, a group of artists formed a club for the purpose of sketching. The members were Chapman, Ingham, Cummings, Durand, Gray, Morton, Edmonds, Agate, Cole, Mount, Casilear, Shegogue, Baker, Prud'homme, Jones and Gignoux. At a designated hour, the company would sit down with everything ready but the "subject." The subject was named, a bell was run and the gentlemen had exactly one hour to make their drawing. At the end of the season, the sketches were exhibited and then distributed to their owners.[41] The club was short-lived, but produced many sketches, some of which are still around. The Karolik Collection in Boston and the New York Public Library have some of Edmonds' sketches (Figures 9, 10). These have been praised for their, "...freshness and immediacy of view."[42]

Edmonds cited his earlier membership in the "XXI" or Sketch Club in his autobiography, along with the names of some of the members.[43] Because the beginnings of the "XXI" or Sketch Club are shrouded in obscurity and because Edmonds' original membership was interrupted by his sojourn in Hudson, we must rely on Cummings who included Edmonds as, "...one of the original or old 'Sketch Club' and as one of the founders of the 'Century Club.'"[44]

---

41) Cummings, op. cit., 175-6.

42) Frank Weitenkampf, American Graphic Art (Revised ed., New York, 1924), 86-8.

43) Edmonds, "Autobiography," III, 17.

44) Cummings, op. cit., 318-9.

The Sketch Club item concluded Edmonds' autobiography. The autobiographies were found in an envelope pasted to the back of a self-portrait. Since the documents were headed "Dear Durand," it is believed that they and the self-portrait, now owned by Francis Edmonds Tyng, had been in Durand's possession and returned to Edmonds' family at some point. They may have been intended for use by Durand, as the then president of the NAD to turn over to H.T. Tuckerman to be used as the basis for his first book.[45]

To recapitulate, Edmonds was one of the prime figures involved in the organization of the Apollo Association in 1839 and its first Treasurer. He was, in fact, one of the leading figures in the city of New York in the promotion of art and was concerned in most cultural activities of the city as well. He remained deeply involved when the Apollo was renamed the American Art-Union and was one of its directors as well as one of its artists.[46] His position was unique in the city at that time. The entire story of the Art-Union and its difficulties may be read elsewhere, but this seems to have been the focal point for the hard feeling that arose between Cummings and Edmonds.

The remainder of the 1840s was very productive, artistically and financially for Edmonds. The NAD exhibit for

---

45) Henry T. Tuckerman, Artist's Life; or Sketches of American Painters (New York, 1847).

46) Cummings, op. cit., 318-9.

1845 carried his New Scholar, Facing the Enemy and the engraving of Sparking by Alfred Jones, destined for Art-Union
distribution. George Templeton Strong, man-about-town,
said that the only paintings worth mentioning that year
were those by Edmonds, Cole and Durand.[47]

Facing the Enemy (Figure 11) was selected by a Temperance Society for engraving and distribution. The Society
compiled a little story for their handbill, describing the
gentleman in the painting as a reformed drunkard.[48] Far
from being reformed, every aspect of the picture, pro-
claims his indecision. As he faces a windowsill on which
stands a partially filled decanter, his chair wavers as it
totters on two legs; his bulbous nose, ruddy complexion and
bleary eye show his proclivities, while an axe in the foreground gives another indication of his dilemma. The oil
sketch for this painting is held by a private collector in
New York. Comparison with Mount's painting of Loss and
Gain (Figure 12), in the collection of Mr. and Mrs. William
Middendorf, II, in New York, emphasizes Edmonds' empathy
for the human dilemma, while Mount has given us only a jolly
drunkard whose sole concern is for the jug beyond his reach.

The New Scholar was exhibited at the American Art-
Union in 1845, too, and a lengthy review praising this work
was found in a compilation of Art-Union clippings at the

47) Allan Nevins & Milton Thomas, eds., The Diary of
George Templeton Strong (New York, 1952), 258.

48) Edmonds Folder, op. cit.

New-York Historical Society. There is no indication who
gathered these reviews, but the large number of clippings
referring to Edmonds' works makes one wonder if he was
responsible for collecting them.

The engraving of the Scholar was distributed by the
AAU to its members in 1850. In it a mother introduces her
small son to the teacher for the first time. While the
small boy's dog is smelling the schoolmaster's legs, the
teacher, with a pen in his mouth, hides a switch behind his
back. The walls and floor contain many appropriate objects and through the open door there is a glimpse of the
schoolroom. A reviewer said, "Simple and unpretending as
is the subject of this picture, it belongs to a class for
which we have a decided passion. It appeals not to the in-
tellect but to the heart...We think it one of the most
original of the artist's design...The arrangement of colors
is agreeable and harmonious, and the general effect of
light and shadow, more concentrated and effective than is
usually the case with this gentleman's pictures."[49]

Not the least interesting facet of this review is what
it had to say about Edmonds, the man:

> Considering the fact that Mr. Edmonds oc-
> cupies the responsible station of a cashier
> in a bank and that in Wall St., too; he en-
> joys a remarkable reputation as an artist.
> His pictures are comparatively few, owing
> to his peculiar situation and the correct
> notion he entertains, that pictures should
> not be exhibited to the public until the

49) Express, AAU Press Book, op. cit., n.d.

artist does his best to make it perfect
...We have never known an individual...
so thoroughly systematic in his employ-
ments. When at the bank he never allows
an individual to converse with him about
art and when in his studio it is but seldom
that he alludes to his legitimate business.
When we consider the brilliancy of his
genius, and his peculiar situation and
manner of life, we are constrained to admire him as one of the most remarkable men
of the day...He is a man of quite extensive reading and expansive mind, and his
pictures are an index to the humor which
it contains...They are generally intended
to make you laugh, but often possess an
undercurrent of philosophy, which makes
them voiceless preachers to the thoughtful
man. We only wish that he was an artist
by profession, and not merely an amateur.[50]

In 1846, in addition to being a Member of the Council
and a Member of the Committee of Arrangements at the NAD,
Edmonds became the Recording Secretary, a post he was to
hold along with the others for the next three years. His
pictures that year were again received with acclaim. One
critic referred to Edmonds as "...undeniably the first
amateur painter in America." After commending Edmonds on
his good taste, the critic went on to describe the manner
in which visitors in general view exhibitions:

At the tragic, swaggering, theatrical-
historical paintings, they yawn; before
some of the grand flash landscapes, they
stand without the least emotion; for in
these same big pictures you often see signs
of ignoranceof every kind; weakness of hand,
poverty of invention, carelessness of drawing, and sometimes lamentable imbecility of
thought; but before some quiet scene of humor
or pathos, some easy little copy of nature,

---

50) Express, AAU Press Book, op. cit., n.d.

you shall see the same visitor stand for
a long time in pleased contemplation. And
this is the test, as we have frequently had
occasion to observe, that Mr. Edmonds' pictures always bear. We once saw two country-
men, restless enough elsewhere in the Academy,
stand for something like an hour, regarding
attentively his rustic sketch of "Sparking."[51]

Three paintings were offered by Edmonds in '46 at the

NAD. Lord Glenallen and Elspeth Macklebackit was the first

literary subject he attempted since his return from Europe.

The NAD catalogue carried the quote from Sir Walter Scott's

Antiquary on which the picture was based, an indication

that Edmonds' interest and admiration for Scott were far

from dead.[52] The N.Y. Mirror described the picture as com-

posed simply of two persons, those named in the title, who,

"...are delineated with great skill and a nice discrimina-

tion of character. All the subordinate parts of the picture

are put in with most admirable effect and finished with a

delicacy of touch which few of our artists attempt."[53]

The Knickerbocker, in addition to praising the picture, noted

the accessories of the cottage, the brass-kettle, the sus-

pended haddock, the "pot of jam" on the shelf, etc. Then,

"Is Elspeth's searching glance directed 'anywhere else' than

at Glenallen? is that warning finger raised at anything save

him? Can his look be mistaken by any body? No; it tells

51) Knickerbocker, XXIX (May 1846), 464.

52) NAD Cat., 1846, #167.

53) New York Mirror, XXIV (May 22, 1846), 92.

the tale."[54] To be able to tell the tale at a glance was
the ultimate criterion and the epitome of success.

The Sleepy Student was very well liked by the same
critic. He mentioned, "The Dog in his lap; the dropped
book; the wash-bench, with its variety and completeness of
utensils and with the no less natural adjuncts underneath;
all are to the life."[55] The reviewer was surprised by the
pleasant landscape Edmonds had entered, but found fault
with a round white cloud. The critic of the N.Y. Mirror
was equally surprised by the landscape, but said that Edmonds, "...exhibits here a genuine love for trees and green
fields."[56] This critic, however, found fault with The
Sleepy Student because the way the light was cast upon the
wall could not happen in nature. It is debatable whether
the critic was correct about the light upon the wall. The
painting, held by an Edmonds' relative in Connecticut, is
especially notable for its golden tone. The critic also
suggested that Cole and Edmonds could profitably form a
partnership, because, "What could be finer than a landscape
by Cole with figures by Mount or Edmonds?"[57]

The only painting submitted by Edmonds to the NAD in
1847 was The Orphan's Funeral. The reviews differed widely.
One critic, who had condemned Edmonds for faulty perspective

54) Knickerbocker, XXIX (May 1846), 464.

55) Knickerbocker, XXIV (May 1846), 464.

56) New York Mirror, XXIV (May 9, 1846), 2.

57) Ibid. (May 22, 1846), 92.

and poor drawing, added, "He is more missed in the exhibition this year than he would have been out of it."[58] Another review, however, said that the painting told its affecting story at a glance. "A young mother is carrying to the grave the coffin of her only and infant child; and 'all the Mother' bereft of her last earthly joy, is expressed in her face...Mr. Edmonds has chose wisely, and with characteristically good judgment, omitted all such accessories as might distract attention from the main object."[59]

1847 was the last year that the <u>Knickerbocker</u> gave Edmonds anything more than a brief mention. The <u>Literary World</u> seemed to take up where the former periodical had left off. Its criticisms of Edmonds' works at the NAD for 1848 could hardly be regarded as laudatory. This was however, the year that the war between the AAU and the NAD was at its peak and the reviewer may very well have had opinions about the strife and its participants that could affect his review:

> ...There is much good color and careful painting in <u>The First Earning</u> (136) but the picture looks empty and the figures want the form of action. They look too artificially posed, too much as if they had been arranged and placed by the artist in order to be painted. Perspective in

---

58) <u>Literary World</u>, I (June 5, 1847), 420.

59) <u>Knickerbocker</u>, XXIX (June 1847), 572.

> Mr. Edmonds' pictures is most shockingly
> out, and in this as in The Trial of
> Patience (223), is so apparently ridicu-
> lous, that it ceases to be even "common-
> sense perspective." This latter picture
> we do not like, though it has many admir-
> able qualities; but the subject is coarse,
> and reminds us too strongly of the vul-
> garities of life. We would rather hear
> it told that women have their patience
> tried, when brutal husbands eject their
> tobacco juice over the just washed linen,
> than see it done or painted. Not even
> the look of sweet reproval the poor wife
> casts upon the offender, will relieve the
> picture from the association of images
> of a disgusting nature.[60]

Trial of Patience could have been inspired by the many

Dutch and Flemish works that Edmonds had seen while abroad.

The subjects of many of these would make Edmonds' picture

seem a pallid affair by comparison. His sympathy for the

lady in the picture might have been inspired by current

events. In 1848, the legislature of the state of New York

passed the first Married Women's Property Law that gave

women certain limited rights in the control of their own

property. The law was passed after 12 years of discussion

that showed that the struggle for women's rights was not a

new thing.[61] The movement received much support and sympa-

thy from the Quakers.[62] Although, no longer a practising

Quaker, Edmonds never lost sympathy for the Friends, nor

was he alienated from their early influence.

---

60) Literary World, III (May 27, 1848), 328.

61) Alice Felt Tyler, Freedom's Ferment (New York, 1962), 460.

62) Ibid., 450-3.

Another opinion on <u>First Earnings</u> is illustrated by the fact that the picture was exhibited at the Pennsylvania Academy of Fine Arts in 1855 by its owners, Stillman and Durand.[63]

In the fall of 1848, Edmonds more than redeemed himself with <u>The Strolling Musician</u> at the AAU. Now in the collection of John J. Heinz, III, of Pittsburgh, Pa., it is titled <u>The Organ-Grinder</u> (Figure 13). The following rave was published in several places:

> A pleasing composition of the Wilkie
> school, in which class of subjects
> Mr. Edmonds chiefly delights, is always
> happy and is known to be unrivalled.
> In this picture we have a rural interior
> with a large group of peasants giving
> audience, after the evening meal to a
> wandering organ-player. The child in
> its mother's lap is excessively taken
> with the "fantastic tricks" of the monkey
> "dressed in a little brief" red coat,
> and a worthy son of Labor is tambouring
> it on the "obverse" of a plate by way of
> accompaniment to the strains of the organ.
> A cheerful picture for a cheerful "house-
> hold room."[64]

The painting was certainly a major effort for Edmonds, with its 12 figures, if you count the monkey. The setting was probably typical of farmhouse interiors of its era, but it comes as a shock to read that these people were regarded as "peasants" when we have prided ourselves on our egalitarianism

---

63) Anna Wells Rutledge, <u>Pennsylvania Academy Cumulative Record of Exhibition Catalogues</u> (Philadelphia, 1955), 68.

64) <u>Town and County</u>, n.v. (Nov. 11, 1848), 2; <u>Commercial Advertiser</u> (Buffalo), Nov. 13, 1848.

for so long. The color is again golden in tone, reminiscent of the color in The Sleepy Student and it has touches of color typical of Edmonds.

A complaint was registered by another reviewer who said, "...Why cannot Edmonds vary his countenance more? The same female face is seen in every one of his pictures..."[65] The AAU Press Book, however, has many more positive reviews of this picture.

Edmonds' only painting for 1849, Gil Blas and the Archbishop, was exhibited at the AAU. Recently rediscovered and now owned by a private collector in New York, it fully merits the praise bestowed upon it then. The approval from the AAU might have been suspect when it said, "Mr. Edmonds' illustration of Gil Blas will delight everybody by its quiet humor as well as its silvery tone. It is stronger in color than his works have generally been, and on many accounts may be pronounced his chef d'ouevre."[66]

The Literary World, however, had not been notably friendly to Edmonds before and it said, "Edmonds has just finished some of his best things for the Art-Union. It represents Gil Blas in the act of passing that unfortunate criticism upon the sermons of his patron, the Archbishop, which cost the poor valet his place. The aspect of complacency with which Gil Blas is uttering his judgment is

65) AAU Press Book, op. cit., New York Day Book, Nov. 20, 1848.

66) AAU Bulletin, I (April 1849), 14.

extremely well contrasted with the expression of utter
contempt for his opinion seen on the face of the ec-
clesiastic...The still life of the picture is admirably
painted and the coloring pleases us more than that of
some of Edmonds' recent works."[67]

Some amplifications on the selection of the topic re-
veals interesting aspects. The Archbishop, in the story
by Lesage, had emphasized over and over to Gil Blas that
the only way to get along in life was by being totally
honest. When Gil Blas expressed his honest opinion to his
mentor, his reward was to be thrown out. Such a wry commentary from Edmonds the banker, might have reflected his
experiences. The negative portrayal of a Catholic religious official could have been a mirror for reactions to
the Nativist movement that reached its peak in 1850. Samuel
F.B. Morse, former president of the NAD and the Episcopalian
Rev. Lyman Beecher were leaders of the Nativist or Know-
Nothing Movement.[68]

The success of the AAU had resulted in a number of exhibitions during the year and it may be noted that Gil Blas
was shown in the spring, in direct competition with the NAD.
John Durand related the incident that took place between
the two groups that brought the whole matter to a head in

---

67) <u>Literary World</u>, IV (March 10, 1849), 228.

68) Richard B. Morris, ed., <u>Encyclopedia of American History</u> (New York, 1961), 187, 218, 584.

the spring of 1848.[69]   In Sept. 1849, Edmonds wrote to
Durand, president of the NAD, in a tone that indicated the
war was over. "I have received the circular and that no
more hard thoughts may be had, I should like to send one
or two of my pictures; but you know all the pictures I
have painted are out of my hands. I want your opinion as
to which of my pictures you would advise me to send. You
know I do not paint enough pictures to give me any great
choice-But I do believe you are familiar with most of them."[70]
From this we deduce that the friendship between the men
stood firm, that Edmonds produced relatively few paintings
and that he sold most of them.

The two pictures for the NAD exhibit of 1850 that Dur-
and helped to select were The Two Culprits and Courtship in
New Amsterdam. A recent photograph from the files of an
art dealer in New York, confirms that the Culprits, now
titled, The Schoolmaster (Figure 14), survives, but its
whereabouts are unknown. The original title and its subject were based on selections from Washington Irving's
Sketchbook that described Ichabod Crane, his practices as
a teacher and the appearance of the schoolroom.[71] The

---

69) Durand, op. cit., 168-171.

70) Durand Papers, op. cit., Edmonds to A.B. Durand,
Sept. 10, 1849.

71) Washington Irving, Sketchbook of Geoffrey Crayon,
Gent., "The Legend of Sleepy Hollow" (New York, n.d.),
270-1.

schoolmaster, a malicious looking pedagogue, holds a ruler
in his hand with which he has apparently just punished one
crying lad, while the other fearfully holds his hand out
for the expected blow. In the background, the other boys
talk and giggle while they watch. The somewhat dingy schoolroom is eloquently shown. The AAU review of the NAD exhibition praised this painting.[72]

The other picture, Courtship in New Amsterdam, may or
may not have been based on the "Legend of Sleepy Hollow,"
too. The Literary World said, "...(it) turns the laugh
upon a Knickerbocker swain of the old school...not in the
best style of the artist-it wants finish and greater attention in the drawing. But the inside of the tin kettle
turned up against the door is in the highest style of
copper...it reflects the housewifery of New Amsterdam to
the great credit of the young 'Vrow' who sits in the doorway..."[73]

Edmonds might not have had the time to properly finish
his work in 1850 because that was the year he moved to
Bronxville. On Oct. 11, 1849, he purchased his first piece
of property in what was then called East Chester and he
purchased his last parcel in 1853.[74] As a director of the
Harlem railroad, he had to be familiar with the service the

---

72) AAU Bulletin, II (May 1850), 448.

73) Literary World, VI (May 4, 1850), 448.

74) Sybil Brush, "The Story Begins with an Artist,"
The Villager, n.v. (March 1966), 2.

line could offer. The needs of his growing family were increasing and, as it was, they had become accustomed to leaving the city each summer.[75] The move to the suburbs had begun, as attested by the popularity of the books by Andrew Jackson Downing. The success of Downing's advocacy of the Gothic for cottages and residences can be seen throughout our country to this day.[76] Before Edmonds was able to build his Gothic cottage, Crow's Nest, he had to provide a graded, cobble-stoned road so oxen could find purchase for their feet as they hauled cartloads of native cut granite to the top. The community was rich in skilled stoneworkers, because recently opened quarries had imported trained workmen from England and Italy.[77]

An original sketch by Edmonds of Crow's Nest, now in a private collection in New York, depicts a relatively modest, two-story Gothic cottage (Figure 15). Edmonds put additions on in 1854, presumably because of the growth of his family.[78] The house as it stands today is a great stone castle of 30 rooms, but renovations were made by later owners.[79]

---

75) Durand Papers, op. cit., Edmonds to A.B. Durand, July, 19, 1849.

76) Wayne Andrews, Architecture, Ambition and Americans (New York, 1967), 107-9.

77) Brush, op. cit., 2.

78) Francis William Edmonds, "Diary 1854." (Possession of author).

79) Brush, op. cit., 6.

Edmonds' preoccupations in Bronxville were reflected
by his showing of the same painting, and no other, at both
the AAU and the NAD in 1851. John Durand wrote to his
father describing a visit to Bronxville and finding Edmonds very upset because a well that had been drilled
through 40 feet of solid rock had not produced water.[80]
Eventually he did find water, because the well is still
there.

The NAD painting by Edmonds in 1851 was called, "What
can a young Lassie do wi' an auld man," from the poems of
Robert Burns. One critic said, "Edmonds' illustration...
where gout and elasticity, imbecility and contempt, are
capitally rendered."[81] The AAU carried the description in
its catalogue. "A feeble old man taking his bowl of gruel,
while his young wife stands at the open window as if impatient of the restraint that kept her at home."[82] The
bulletin included a wood cut based on the picture of the
young lady looking mournfully out the window, while the
rather horrible old man spoons up his gruel. Burns' verse
was quoted in full, accentuating how well Edmonds had cap-
tured the idea of the poem. Oddly enough, Cowdrey missed
listing this picture in her exhibition record.[83]

---

80) Durand Papers, op. cit., John Durand to A.B.
Durand, Sept. 8, 1851.

81) Literary World, VIII (April 19, 1851), 320.

82) Cowdrey, op. cit., II, 128.

83) Ibid.

The Speculator, offered by Edmonds at the NAD in 1852, received mixed reviews (Figure 16). One said that the faces were "coarse and conventional" and another that they were too much alike. They agreed that the accessories were extremely well done, to the point where one critic claimed he had been almost tempted to draw the cork from a demijohn under the table.[84] The evils of speculation were an early concern for Edmonds. In 1838, he drew a sketch, The Paper City (Figure 17), now at the New-York Historical Society, Accession No. 1944.386, that referred to the practice of constructing so-called cities in anticipation of expected inhabitants.[85] When Edmonds wrote to Flagg in 1843, regarding the organization of the New York and Erie railroad, he made it very clear that he was concerned with his own probity and the evils of speculation. The oil sketch for this picture, owned by a relative in Connecticut, lacking only the faces, shows the verve Edmonds was capable of and his use of color.

The Speculator, titled The Real Estate Agent was purchased by Charles Wilson who presented it to President Eisenhower in 1956.[86] Eisenhower presented it to someone else a year later who eventually returned it to Eisenhower.

---

84) Literary World, X (May 1, 1952), 316; Town and Country, n.v. (May 8, 1852), 2.

85) Christopher Tunnard & Henry H. Reed, American Skyline (New York, 1956), 94.

86) Edmonds Folder, op. cit., News clipping.

•

Somewhere in the course of the last transaction the painting was lost, so its present location is unknown.[87]

The last painting that Edmonds painted for the AAU,
prior to its demise was Preparing for Christmas. The
catalogue describes it as: "Two men in the open air, before a stable, are picking turkeys for the kitchen; a negro
is blowing his hands to keep them warm. The ground is
covered with snow."[88]

In 1851, and for the next eight years, Edmonds was
listed as Treasurer, Member of the Council and the Committee of Arrangements. Cummings betrayed his spite against
Edmonds, when, in the list of officers in the Annals, he
added in parentheses after Edmonds' name as Treasurer that
it was "(nominally, during Mr. Cumming's occupancy of the
Vice-Presidency)."[89]

The decision of the Court of Appeals against the Art-
Union's mode of distribution to the effect that it "...was
illegal and unconstitutional" would seem to have ended the
year on a pessimistic note. And, in fact, although its
managers tried nobly, it never recovered.[90]

---

87) Mrs. D.D. Eisenhower correspondence with author.

88) Cowdrey, AAU, II, op. cit., 128.

89) Cummings, op. cit., Appendix.

90) Cowdrey, AAU, I, op. cit., 223-240.

CHAPTER V

Banking Problems and Art, 1853-1855

Edmonds was one of the two men credited with the organization of the first full-fledged American clearing house in 1853. He took the initiative toward the founding of the New York Clearing House and the achievement was recognized by his being made the chairman of the first clearing house committee.[1] George D. Lyman published a proposal in the Journal of Commerce that daily balances be settled through a special agency at a designated place, using a method other than the physical transference of coin.[2] Lyman ultimately had the opportunity to explain his suggestions to a few New York bank leaders, one of whom, Thomas Tileston came to see its possibilities.[3]

"While Lyman's suggestions were still in the stage of discussion under the chairmanship of Thomas Tileston, a small group of bank cashiers led by Edmonds was taking action."[4] Edmonds seemed to have worked on the basis of a plan devised

---

1) Redlich, op. cit., II, 48-9.

2) Ibid., Footnote 34, 49.

3) Ibid., 50.

4) Ibid.

by James C. Hallock, Sr., who went from bank to bank between the fall of 1852 and the spring of 1853 promoting
his ideas.[5] In 1852, possibly under the influence of
Hallock, Edmonds induced four other banks to join with
the Mechanics' Bank in organizing a new system of settle-
ments. All five banks contributed to a $1,000,000 fund
in coin which was deposited with the Mechanics' Bank.
This bank issued coin certificates, devised by Edmonds, to
aid the five associated banks in the settlement of their
daily balances. This saved, not only the trouble of count-
ing the coin repeatedly, but the risk and physical effort
of moving it back and forth.[6]

In April 1853, the two groups joined forces and Edmonds called a meeting of bank officers. The necessity for
some change was clear, so a committee of bank cashiers was
appointed with Edmonds as chairman. The first American
clearing house opened in New York on Oct. 11, 1853 with
Lyman as its manager. The New York Clearing House was at
first an informal organization directed ostensibly by the
cashier's committee, but actually by its chairman, Francis
William Edmonds.[7]

The initial successes of the clearing house were the
result of contributions by the members of various age

5) Redlich, op. cit., II, 50.

6) Ibid.

7) Ibid., 49-50.

groups. Lyman, the idea man, was about thirty; the cashiers, including Edmonds, were in their forties and provided the driving power, but the plan could not have succeeded without the personal and professional prestige of men in their sixties like Thomas Tileston.[8]

Edmonds' diary of 1854 had many references to the clearing house. It seems to have been a bad year financially, stocks were falling and many banks were in trouble. The inability to pay their balances caused the suspension of several banks from the clearing house during the year.[9] A note in the diary reads, "Clamor against me as being instrumental in breaking banks."[10] Edmonds' position was evidently recognized in terms of both blame and praise.

Edmonds had been appointed City Chamberlain for 1854 and at the beginning of 1855, the Mayor-Elect Fernando Wood sent in Edmonds' nomination for '55.[11] Edmonds seems to have set great store by this position, yet it was a political appointment having little to do with merit. The president of the Mechanics' Bank, Shepherd Knapp, a Whig, managed to become the city chamberlain, while Edmonds a Democrat, was a member of the opposition party.[12] Knapp

8) Redlich, op. cit., II, 50.

9) Francis William Edmonds, "Diary 1854," Oct. 9, Dec. 9.

10) Ibid., Dec. 13.

11) Edmonds, "Diary 1854," Jan. 2, 1855.

12) Edmonds, "Defence," op. cit., 23.

lost his appointment when the Democrats won the election in 1853, but Edmonds succeeded him. The anxiety to retain the appointment was related to the idle funds of the City of New York, because no interest had to be paid on city deposits which, however, could be utilized in making loans to bank customers.[13]

Throughout 1854, Edmonds noted his frequent meetings with City Comptroller Azariah Flagg, the same Flagg who held the same position earlier for the state of New York. These meetings were necessitated by Edmonds' position as Chamberlain in handling the monies of the city. Each time he met with the Governor and other high dignitaries of the state and city, he found it important enough to record.

Edmonds' diary is so equally divided between business events and personal events that it is easy to see they might have been all one to him. Another direct result of his positions as Cashier and Director was many other directorships. This business practice brings a modest emolument for attendance at director's meetings and is still practiced. However, some of Edmonds' interests were deeper than that, as with the Erie and Harlem railroads. During 1854, he made constant references to the condition of the Erie stock and quoted its exchange rate very often. When the Erie made an application for a loan, it was Edmonds who called the meeting of the Directors. After the loan

13) Redlich, op. cit., II, 49.

was granted, the Erie stock began to move up, with Edmonds
still keeping track.[14]

Along with all the references to the panic in Wall
Street, bank failures, defalcations by tellers and frauds
by others, Edmonds unfolded a story of how a gentleman
farmer lived in Bronxville. At the same time, he was hard
at work having the house enlarged by a two floor extension
to the original house and a third story addition over all.
By the time he finished, except for minor additions, Crow's
Nest had become the thirty room stone castle it is today.

Besides the workmen who were performing the work on
the house, there were a number of men who worked Edmonds'
small farm, whose produce graced his table in season. In
the spring, asparagus was plentiful, followed by straw-
berries and so on. For example, "Tom, Enoch & Patrick at
work on potatoes, finished digging & got in 104 baskets,
about 80 bushels, good potatoes, too."[15]

There was constant allusion throughout the year to the
servant problem, involving frequent replacements. For a
change of pace that year, the entire family of two adults,
four children and a servant came to New York for several
week during Lent. They stayed at a hotel, the Collamore
House, at a rate of $60 a day, including board, that covered
all seven of them.[16] Edmonds hated hotel living so much

14) Edmonds, "Diary 1854," Aug. 24-5, Sept. 2, 13.

15) Ibid., Sept. 9.

16) Ibid., Mar. 7.

that when they came down for the Christmas season they
stayed with Josephine Hilton.

In spite of all this activity, neither the pursuance
of his painting nor his artistic acquaintances were
neglected. He attended the Sketch Club, the Century Club
and visited his artist friends, mostly Casilear, but also
Durand and Kensett. Mrs. Edmonds visited the Durand family,
too. John Durand and Casilear were both frequent visitors
in Bronxville. While in the city, Edmonds attended various
artistic events with Leupp and Cozzens.

Edmonds only exhibited one painting at the NAD for
each year in 1853 and 1854, but his diary makes it clear
that he executed others. On July 25th, he varnished two
pictures, but gave no clue as to what they were. He did
a pencil sketch of a neighbor's dying child.[17] Painting
or sketching portraits of the dead or dying was common
practice for nineteenth century artists.[18] Later in the
year, he worked on the portrait of a friend identified only
as "Tiffany."[19] The Tiffany family were close friends who
visited with Edmonds and his family almost every weekend
during the summer. This may have been the founder of
Tiffany & Co., who had a store in the Wall Street area at
that time, not L.C. Tiffany, who was too young. Based on
this diary and a number of self-portraits that exist, the

17) Edmonds, "Diary 1854," April 29.

18) Frankenstein, "Mount," op. cit., 26.

19) Edmonds, "Diary 1854," Dec. 25.

presumption is that Edmonds did at least some portraits
every year.

The only picture Edmonds exhibited at the NAD in 1853
was #154, A Passage from Burns. The catalogue carried the
following verse:

> To daunton me and me so young,
> Wi his fause heart and flattering tongue;
> That is the thing you ne'er shall see,
> For an auld man shall never daunton me.

Another picture by Edmonds was exhibited by its owner, J.
Claghorne, in 1853 at the Pennsylvania Academy of Fine
Arts, but there is no clue to when it was painted.[20] Its
title was The First Step, but there are no descriptions for
either painting.

Taking the Census (Figure 18) was exhibited at the
NAD in 1854 and Edmonds recorded both the opening and his
attendance with Mrs. Edmonds.[21] On three separate occasions,
he had mentioned working on the painting in his diary and
made other references to hanging the picture for exhibition. Oddly enough, he says not one word about the very
favorable reception the work received. After discussing
Mount's Bargaining for A Horse, the critic went on:

> A production of the same class is No. 162,
> "Taking the Census" by F.W. Edmonds. Here
> we have represented the census-taker, with
> an important official air, noting down the
> family statistics; his assistant, a lad
> standing in business-like attitude, and all

---

20) Rutledge, op. cit., 68.

21) Edmonds, "Diary 1854," op. cit., Mar. 22, 23.

> alive with the novelty of the occasion;
> farmer----, rough and awkward, reckoning
> in brown study the number of "the boys
> and the girls:" evidently more at home in
> the use of the ox-gad, which lies on the
> floor, than in "figuring"-and so on through
> nine figures, each one of which is a
> character and a triumph. Why has this ad-
> mirable artist treated us to but one picture
> in this collection?[22]

The reviewer obviously accepted this painting, now in

private hands in New York, as totally humorous, but its

sombre coloring, the dull, apathetic stare of the mother

holding an odd-looking baby and one child almost totally

hidden from view, questions if Edmonds had another intent.

Edmonds' career as a banker was dealt a major blow

when in August 1855, a charge of embezzlement against him

was published in the newspapers.[23] The charges coming on

the heels of a year of defalcations, failures and bank

frauds might have been readily accepted by a business com-

munity hardened by a difficult year, but it devastated his

friends in the art world.

Redlich considered this important enough to go into

in detail. He described Edmonds as, "An honest man, an ef-

ficient manager with an excellent reputation and, above all,

an entrepreneur with a creative touch..."[24] Redlich con-

tinued:

> Edmonds' downfall throws an interesting
> light on the way in which reliable American

---

22) _Town and Country_, n.v. (April 1, 1854), 2.

23) Edmonds, "Defence," _op. cit._, 26.

24) Redlich, _op. cit._, 49.

banks were run in the middle of the nineteenth century: The accounting methods
were worse than loose; they were supposed
to have enabled Edmonds to circulate to his
private gain notes of the bank already with-
drawn and to take loans without interest.
It is immaterial whether these charges were
or were not substantiated; that such charges
could be publicly preferred against and
answered by an officer of a reputable bank
is in itself an astonishing fact...both men
(Knapp and Edmonds) made contributions to
their respective parties, and since such
contributions were considered to be in the
bank's interest, the money went from the
general cash into the cashier's draw and
disappeared without being accounted for.
As it happened, one day the bank hired an
assistant cashier who was either unaccustomed to such loose methods or who wanted
the post of cashier for himself. He brought
the situation into the open and immediately
Knapp took a strong stand against Edmonds
which may have been motivated by jealousy.
Thus Edmonds had to leave the bank under
suspicion of being a swindler. In reality
he was merely easy-going and careless,
probably identifying himself with his enterprise to such an extent that he lost sight
of the fact that the bank had an indivi-
duality of its own.[25]

Redlich concluded: "This end to Edmonds' career, however,
does not detract from his great merit."[26]

Edmonds' diary of 1854 substantiates a great many of
Redlich's surmises and adds some facts. The entire matter
probably came to light as a result of the reorganization of
the Mechanics' Bank that took place during 1854, to go into
effect, January 1, 1855. Edmonds was in charge of the details and filled his diary with the events throughout the

---

25) Redlich, op. cit., 49.

26) Ibid.

year. Knapp was apparently away from the bank very often,
so the duties and responsibilities of acting president fell
on Edmonds.[27] His salary was raised during one of Knapp's
frequent absences, enraging the latter gentleman who
promptly saw to it that his salary was raised, too.[28] This
casts a shadow on Knapp's later statement that he had
voluntarily relinquished $2000 of his own salary to Ed-
monds.[29] The diary mentioned sums loaned and disbursed
without distinction, as though it all belonged to Edmonds.
Closer examination indicates that most of these funds were
probably from the clearing house or the bank.

Although Edmonds resigned as cashier, he did not give
up his post as Director, stating to the depositors that he
intended to watch over their interests as well as his own,
at least for the remainder of his term. His intention was
to leave the bank forever and devote, "...the rest of my
days to a pursuit far more congenial to me-the pursuit of
the fine arts."[30]

Examination of the diary makes it quite clear that
Edmonds was well able to weather storm financially. He
had dividends coming in from many sources.[31] In addition,

---

27) Edmonds, "Defence," op. cit., 17.

28) Edmonds, "Diary 1854," op. cit., Feb. 18, 20, 25.

29) Shepherd Knapp, Letter to the Stockholders of
the Mechanics' Bank (New York, 1855), 5.

30) Edmonds, "Defence," op. cit., 54.

31) Edmonds, "Diary 1854," op. cit., For example,
Feb. 27, May 2.

he owned a house on Irving Place that he rented for $1000
a year, with a proviso that he was permitted to reserve a
room for over night use.[32]

John Durand wrote to his father about the embezzlement
accusation. "I presume before this you will have read in
the paper about the difficulty between Mr. Edmonds and the
Mechanics' Bank. He has resigned his place. Nelson will
tell you all about it...I refer you to him."[33] Asher
answered his son a few days later. "The astounding matter
...concerning our old friend 'comes indeed' like a 'blight
over my spirits' and spreads a gloom and sadness over all
around me. I will not dwell on it."[34]

E.D. Nelson, pursued the matter in a letter to Durand,
on August 27:

> The Edmonds matter is settling down gently,
> and be the actual truth what it may, Mr.
> Edmonds will not lose position. He is con-
> sidered a victim to personal feeling and for
> the sake of Burke the assistant cashier ob-
> taining his place. Indeed Burke has been
> foolish enough to write a letter to Edmonds
> asking his aid to obtain the vacant cashier-
> ship-an impolitic move on Burke's part as he
> can with very ill grace explore Mr. Edmonds
> as a rogue after asking his aid to obtain an
> office. This places the matter in the very
> best light for Edmonds and his friends are
> willing to let it rest forever.[35]

---

32) Edmonds, "Diary 1854," op. cit., Feb. 24.

33) Durand Papers, op. cit., J. Durand to A.B. Durand,
Aug. 7, 1855.

34) Ibid., A.B. Durand to J. Durand, Aug. 12, 1855.

35) Ibid., E.D. Nelson to A.B. Durand, Aug. 27, 1855.

There are no further personal papers written by Edmonds, other than a few letters. It would have been interesting to see if the frequent headaches and problems with his eyes that plagued him after his initial breakdown in 1840 was aggravated. His complaints in 1854 were dealt with by glasses for the first time, but this was probably due to the normal farsightedness that age brings.

Prior to all the bank difficulties, Edmonds had begun an active involvement within the Episcopalian church. It was to provide a major artistic inspiration, too. Quite early in '54, he was elected Vestryman at St. Paul's Episcopal Church, Eastchester.[36] In this capacity he attended meetings, despite his busy schedule. Later that year he accepted the nomination as delegate to the Episcopal Convention in New York.[37] The convention was held at the end of September and a month later he made his first drawing for "Felix and Paul."[38] The New York Times carried an article that mentioned a controversy in regard to Bishop Onderdonk, at the convention.[39] This significantly ties the painting finally titled, Felix Trembled, to Episcopalian matters.

---

36) Edmonds, "Diary 1854," op. cit., Apr. 19.

37) Ibid., Sept. 19.

38) Ibid., Oct. 30.

39) New York Times, Sept. 30, 1854.

CHAPTER VI

"Felix Trembled"

Felix Trembled was one of the few pictures intended
specifically to be hung inside an antebellum American
Protestant church. Created as an altar piece for St. Paul's
Episcopalian Church, East Chester, N.Y., it was taken down
in the 1930s when the church was designated as an historic
landmark and restored to its colonial appearance. The
painting, which had been hung in 1855 was then rolled up
and stored in the church basement until its recent recovery
and restoration. Now that this large and colorful work has
been restored so that it may be appreciated, research has
revealed that the topic was chosen from the life of St. Paul
because of its particular reference to unjust persecution.
At the time the painting was hung, feelings had been running
very high in the Episcopalian community of New York against
the alleged unjust persecution of their suspended bishop,
Benjamin Tredwell Onderdonk. Certain unresolved tensions
in the painting were due as much to the difficulties inherent
in the topic as to the complexities in the nature of the
artist.

Although the Edmonds painting is not signed, there is
no question of its authenticity, not only because it never

left the church until it was recently sold, but also because of a photograph of the picture in its place over
the altar that may even have been taken at the time of its
installation (Figure 19). There are notes from Edmonds'
diary of 1854 that he wrote at Crow's Nest. The first item
was written on October 19th, "...measure window in East C.
church." The next was on October 30th. "Drawing for my
picture of Felix and Paul!" On the 9th of November he
brought up canvas for the picture and on the 10th he said,
"2 of Decheaux men came up and put up my big canvas for
Paul before Felix to int 12 feet by 9 ft." The last item
was on November 13th, "...painted in morning on Paul and
Felix-small sketch." These were the only references to
the painting in the diary which gives no clues as to how
the topic was selected. Nevertheless, this rare painting
was designed in this early period, to be hung within the
church.

Even as late as 1855, art inside an American Protestant
church, regardless of how noble the subject, was still a
rarity. Protestant Americans had long accepted the ban as
part of their American heritage. Our most eminent authori-
ties in America have always believed that the Puritan
vision of the ideal world of faith was embodied only in
words, books or sermons, because concrete images like paint
ing were "papistical."[1] But the Puritan ban on art also

1) Richardson, op. cit., 29.

arose out of ignorance and lack of usage. The England that the 17th century Puritans left behind had no art schools, art academies or national competitions in art and its artists retained only the education and position of master craftsmen. Puritans banned art only if it seemed immoral, was placed within a church or if the cost appeared extravagant. Thus, the Puritan silence about art in America was a consequence, not a cause of the artistic vacuum.[2]

The ban, however, left an inheritance that was interpreted as hostile to art and left inhibitions that were difficult to overcome. The early 19th century American visitors to Europe, finding themselves aroused by the splendors of Catholic art, kept a watchful eye on the emotions that were provoked. John Adams said that the fine arts could never be enlisted in the cause of virtue and piety because "From the dawn of history they have been prostituted to the service of superstition and despotism..."[3] Although Edmonds' visit to Rome in 1841 was quite a bit later, his American reaction to Catholicism was still stiffnecked. While waiting in the streets of Rome he came upon the Pope and his retinue. In his travel journal he recorded how everyone behaved, kneeling, scraping, etc, but "I did not even doff my beaver, but only nodded slightly."[4] An

2) Harris, op. cit., 4-5.

3) Ibid., 36.

4) Edmonds, "Travel Journal," op. cit., Jan. 19, 1841.

American Protestant continued to be wary of "popery." But
the growth of romanticism in antebellum America was to provide the way to break down the Puritan hostility to art in
general, even if not to Catholicism in particular.

The romantic movement with its rebellion against reason
brought a revival of Christianity at the very beginning of
the 19th century. Americans embraced romanticism in many
forms, but their pragmatic natures were ill at ease with
some of its facets. Transcendentalism, the peculiar American form of religious romanticism, was detached from tradi-
tional Christianity, but its association with nature made
it respectable. Painters "turned to the Bible as a store-
house for imaginative inspiration for art, but not for
liturgical pictures: for the churches made little or no
use of them. Their religious painting were made for the
layman and the exhibition gallery, not for the altar."[5]

As a result, there was a wide range of paintings.
Benjamin West chose Saul and the Witch of Endor as early as
1777, a topic repeated by William Sidney Mount in 1828.
William Dunlap painted Christ Rejected in 1822, basing it
on a printed description of a West picture on the same subject. Washington Allston produced the contemplative Elijah
in the Desert in 1818.[6] But as European travel became more
practical and popular, the knowledge grew that art objects

---

5) Richardson, op. cit., 142.

6) Ibid., 142-148.

were powerful means of bringing men to God.[7]

The romantic movement affected Christianity in England in a positive way when the Oxford Movement caused the refurbishing and beautifying of churches that had fallen into disuse and disorder. The Oxford Movement that began in England in 1832 found ready acceptance within the American Episcopalian church, the American version of the Church of England. The first impact could be seen in church architecture in both countries. In America, "the Gothic seemed appropriate for religious architecture because it had less finish and definition than classical forms: its fragmentary, tentative qualities suggested the infinite, as religious buildings were expected to."[8] The recommendations for interior decoration were accepted much more slowly when they were accepted at all.

Nevertheless, by 1857 the Crayon was able to run an article that attempted to prove that prejudice against the use of "Art" for religious purposes was dying away. The Crayon cited a pamphlet by the Rev. Morgan Dix entitled "Plea for the use of the Fine Arts in the Decoration of Churches." Dix said that the general views advanced in the treatise:

> are commended to the careful attention of
> all those enlightened persons, of what-
> ever persuasion, who love the Fine Arts,
> who believe that the mission of the artist

---

7) Harris, op. cit., 134.

8) Ibid., 136.

is a sacred one, and who desire to see the
relation of Art and Religion placed on its
true basis in our young and vigorous country.[9]

The countless beautiful church edifices throughout the coun-

try were mentioned and the pamphlet ended with the follow-

ing note:

St. Paul's Church, East Chester, has an
oil-painting, the subject of which is St.
Paul before Felix. The time chosen by the
artist is when "Felix Trembled." There are
six figures, a little larger than life. The
size of the picture is twelve feet high by
nine feet wide. It was painted expressly
for the church by Mr. F.W. Edmonds.[10]

The _Crayon_ went on to summarize the other art to be found

inside churches: "...the Church of the Annunciation in

this city possesses a large bas-relief, by Mr.H.K. Brown,

the subject being the Annunciation...several designs by

Mr. R.W. Weir for windows in Calvary Church and Trinity

Chapel. Mr. Weir has also painted a picture for the Church

of the Holy Cross at Troy, and one for St. Clement's Church

in this city."[11]

Of the oil paintings, only the "Felix" remains and

only the window at Calvary of the other works. The bas-

relief was destroyed when the building was torn down and

the windows at Trinity Chapel were destroyed by a bomb

blast in their neighborhood. The windows at Calvary may

---

9) The Crayon, IV (Sept. 1857), 288.

10) _Ibid._

11) _Ibid._

still be seen. A centennial history of the church, written
in 1936, said of the 1847 designs, "Weir was at West Point
when he transferred his designs for the Calvary windows
and painted them upon glass. The paint has corroded during the years...but the force and fascination of the picture of the Empty Cross, with the Easter sun coming up
upon it and the serpent in one of the windows to the left
is undimmed..."[12] The force of the Empty Cross still holds,
but the total impact is diminished by the sentimentality
of the Victorian angels. The pictures that Weir gave to
St. Clements and the Church of the Holy Cross seem to have
been the originals for the windows because the descriptions
correspond. The topics were the "Descent from the Cross"
and the "Ascension" and the pictures are long since gone.
Felix Trembled, a very different kind of religious painting remains.

The story of Paul before Felix is from the Acts and
it explains why Felix trembled.[13] Edmonds' treatment of
the topic suggests that his Quaker inhibitions were still
strong enough so that he approached the topic more as a
genre painter out to "tell the story" rather than intent
on depicting a religious story. An eminent art historian
has said that he has never before seen this particular topic

12) Samuel M. Shoemaker, Calvary Church, Yesterday,
Today, A Centennial History (New York, 1936), 70-1.

13) Acts: 21-25.

illustrated.[14] It was painted just four years prior to
Edmonds' version by Jared B. Flagg and exhibited at the
NAD in 1851. Flagg was studying for an Episcopalian priest-
hood then and was ordained in 1855.[15] This is another link
in the evidence that suggests the painting is tied to the
case of Bishop Benjamin Tredwell Onderdonk.

The incident on which the painting was based took
place about 60 A.D. when Felix was Procurator of Judea.
His wife, depicted in the painting, was Drusilla, a Jewess,
daughter of Herod Agrippa. She deserted her husband,
Azizus, King of Emesa, to marry Felix without sanction in
an adulterous union. Paul, attempting to preach Christianity to the Jews in the Temple, was rescued by the Romans
from the mob that attacked him. Paul was bound in chains
and brought before Felix. Felix released Paul from chains
because he was a Roman citizen, but kept him in custody for
two years. During that time, he constantly summoned Paul
to appear before him as a means of harassment and with the
hope that this would bring bribery money from Paul to effect his release. "Felix Trembled" when Paul preached of
righteousness (condemning Felix's receipt of bribes and
evil government), of continence (with special reference to
the adulterous union of Drusilla and Felix), and of the
final judgment, which will be without respecter of persons.

---

14) Professor H.W. Janson to author, Nov. 11, 1971.

15) Groce and Wallace, op. cit., 230.

The result was that although Felix trembled, he delayed his repentance, and that Drusilla became an irreconcileable enemy of Paul.[16] Felix did not release Paul, but passed him on to another jurisdiction where Paul continued to be imprisoned.

The first piece of evidence to link the painting to the case of Bishop Onderdonk was the photograph of the interior of the church with the picture in its place over the altar. Canon West placed this as "high" Episcopalian and linked the theme of unjust persecution to Onderdonk.[17] From the time the Bishop of New York, Benjamin Tredwell Onderdonk, was tried in an ecclesiastical court in 1845 on charges of immorality and impurity, he was regarded as the victim of unjust persecution by an ever larger group in the Episcopalian church. His trial was widely publicized in the popular press of the day in what has been called, "The most notorious in our ecclesiastical annals."[18]

The case arose out of the impact that the Oxford Movement had upon the Episcopalian church, splitting it three ways. The majority of the parish were of the "broad" group or apathetic. The most vituperative group was the "low"

---

16) Rev. D.J. Dummelow, Commentary on the Bible (New York, 1958), Acts: 21-25.

17) Canon Edward N. West, Th. D., sub-dean of the Cathedral Church of St. John the Divine, to author, May 21, 1971.

18) George E. DeMille, The Catholic Movement in the Episcopal Church (Philadelphia, 1950), 63.

church group who thought that Onderdonk had been too partial to elements of the "high" church. Unable to attack
him on ecclesiastical grounds, they chose to effect their
aims this way. The bishop was found guilty, but suspended
so that no sentence could be passed. The suspension was
never revoked and the hard feelings stirred up by the controversy did not abate until the Bishop's death in 1861.[19]

The summation of the evidence that ties <u>Felix Trembled</u>
to the Onderdonk case shows it to be substantial. The
identification of St. Paul's as a "high" Episcopalian
church and the linkage of the theme of unjust persecution
of St. Paul to Onderdonk have come from a scholar within
the Episcopalian church.[20] The selection of the same
topic by Jared Flagg, studying to be an Episcopalian priest,
is especially pointed in view of the fact that we do not
know of this topic ever having been illustrated by other
artists. The Onderdonk case was not only a cause celebre
in its day, but is still being discussed in contemporary
journals. In the 1850s, Onderdonk was held to be a living
martyr by his adherents in his religious community.

It is not known whether Edmonds or Father Coffey, the
priest at St. Paul's suggested the topic, but it was Edmonds who offered to design and execute a painting for St.
Paul's to cover the large East window that was twelve feet

19) See Appendix.

20) Canon West, <u>op. cit.</u>

high by nine feet wide.[21] As far as has been ascertained,
the only other religious painting by Edmonds was a <u>Sermon
on the Mount</u> presented by Edmonds' daughter Grace to St.
Paul's in 1934. This has been lost.[22]

Father Coffey described the reaction of the congrega-
tion to the installation of the picture. "In 1865, who
that lived in those days when that ugly East window with
it's countless panes disappeared entirely covered from
view by that so valued production of Art, the picture of
St. Paul before Felix. I say how can any such one now
living forget the unbounded pleasure which was universally
far and wide felt in this community."[23] If the topic was
linked to Onderdonk, as we believe, then how much greater
must have been the pleasure for the community who thought
they were supporting a martyr.

The first reaction that comes on viewing this painting
for the first time is the sheer pleasure evoked by its rich
and vibrant colors. From the very beginning, Edmonds greatest preoccupation was with color. In this painting he was
able to utilize some of his visual experiences from his
1841 trip abroad. Delacroix had been painting his evoca-
tions of the Near East since 1837 and we know from Edmonds

21) Father Samuel William Coffey, <u>Commemorative Dis-
course</u>, Oct. 24, 1865 (St. Paul's Episcopal Church, Eastchester, N.Y.).

22) Records, St. Paul's Episcopal Church, Eastchester,
N.Y.

23) Father William Samuel Coffey, "Notes" (St. Paul's
Episcopal Church, Eastchester, N.Y.), 2.

journal that he saw a number of them.[24] Here Edmonds used color, not only to emphasize the exotic locale, but also as a compositional device to carry the eye back and forth across the canvas. He made Paul the point to which the eye constantly returned by giving Paul one entire leg of the triangular plan, where he is framed against the light for still greater emphasis and probably to denote Paul's saintliness as well. The background of the Renaissance-style architecture and drape so beloved of the early 19th century history painters, the steps that are angled towards Paul and the vari-colored tile floor are additional devices to direct the eye ever and again towards Paul as he stands with his arms up and outstretched before the five other figures that are grouped together facing him.

The figure of Paul with his somewhat wooden stance can be traced to the influence of Raphael. In April 1841, Edmonds sent home "two lots of small outlines by Raphael." This, in spite of his deprecation of American artists who he heard "lauding Raphael and his followers to the skies and condemning Michael Angelo."[25] But perhaps Edmonds had not changed his mind at all. The figure of Felix is most certainly derived from Michaelangelo and it is the most human figure in the picture. The seated figure

_____

24) Edmonds, "Travel Journal," op. cit., May 16, 23, 1841.

25) Edmonds, "Travel Journal," op. cit., Mar. 7, 1841.

resembles Marius in Vanderlyn's neo-classical "Marius in
the Ruins of Carthage," but they can both be seen to have
origins in the Sistine Chapel ceiling. One might infer
the influence of Ingres in the set of Drusilla's head, but
we can neither prove it nor disprove it.

From the history of the painting, it is clear that
Paul was meant to be the most important figure, but just
as the eye is drawn towards him it is also drawn away from
him. Drusilla is the center of the group that faces Felix
and her face and shoulders have the strongest highlights
of all. The primary colors in her jewelry have the bright-
est hues and she shines out against the dark background
before which she is seated. Standing behind her and a
little to one side is a beautiful and modest handmaiden
who may have been put there to contrast with Drusilla's
more brazen aspect.

Felix is placed forefront diagonally across from Paul.
In its own way this figure is very strong, pulling attention away from all the others. Felix was painted as a
virile figure and with sympathy. The symbols of Rome at
his feet, the sword, shield and helmet with its cockade
of "Edmonds red," proclaim that Felix has the strength of
Rome to support him. It seems as though Edmonds found his
sympathies were again with the human dilemma. Many of
Edmonds previous topics resulted from his sympathy for this
human kind of problem and he often presented them as un-
solvable.

In _Facing the Enemy_, Edmonds put his sot on a teeter-
ing chair with an axe in the foreground while the supposedly
reformed drunkard contemplated the bottle on the window
sill. "What Can a Young Lassie Do Wi' an Auld Man?"
pictured a feeble old man taking his bowl of gruel while
his young wife stands at the open window as if impatient
of the restraint that kept her at home.[26] These were some
of the dilemmas arising out of the human condition that
Edmonds found to be suitable subjects for his brush. They
serve to illustrate his sympathetic approach that did not
provide pat answers in an era that provided nothing else
but. The desire to perfect human institutions had caused
a spate of social reform movements. The American reformer
felt peculiarly free to experiment in his homeland where
there was room and hospitality for his adventure. Education, temperance, universal peace, prison reform, the
rights of women, the evils of slavery, the dangers of
Catholicism, all were legitimate fields for his efforts.[27]

Edmonds had responded to some of these movements and
"Felix" was yet another response. The painting does not
indicate that there was an easy, dogmatic solution possible
to the human condition. Edmonds did not discuss his feelings in writing as a rule, but once in Milan he showed that
he was bothered. "Saw some queer things out of my window-

26) Cowdrey, _AAU_, _op. cit._, I, 128.

27) Tyler, _op. cit._, 2-3.

which rather worked upon my feelings!-Poor thing I feel
sorry for her x x x x"[28]

Finally, the finish of the painting is as detailed as
any of the works that Edmonds exhibited. Despite the huge
size of the canvas, he worked in his usual, fine, tight
manner and so capably that despite the rough treatment the
canvas has received it remains largely in good condition.
It is too bad that no drawings for this huge work were
found. His preliminary work has a spontaneity that is
often preferable to the more highly finished painting.

"Felix Trembled" emerges as an American minor master-
piece that triumphs over its own difficulties because of
the unique American experience that shaped it although
the European influences are readily detected. The American origin is clearly seen in the unusual topic, a selection that arose in an era of romanticism, and the American
passion to espouse the cause of the underdog. Edmonds'
sensibilities produced a richly colored work in keeping
with his temperament, but one that missed a greater mark
because he could not abandon his early religious inhibitions. We are fortunate that this rare work, inspired
by injustice, survives.

---

28) Edmonds, "Travel Journal," op. cit., May 5,
1841.

CHAPTER VII

Final Years and Conclusion

Presumably, the loss of his position as bank cashier
left a void in Edmonds' life which he endeavored to fill
with a new business venture in engraving. He formed an
engraving partnership with Alfred Jones in 1857 and later
the same year they became Edmonds, Jones and Smillie.[1]
The latter firm called itself The Bank Note Engraving
Company. Edmonds not only had the bank-note experience
from banking and financial ability, but presumably had con-
nections in the banking world as well. Jones and Smillie
were fine engravers who had been cast adrift when the
American Art-Union expired. The American Bank Note Company
started a large merger in 1858 that assimilated almost
every engraving firm and skilled engraver in New York City.
According to the chart that was embodied in the Griffith
book on this company's beginnings, the Bank Note Engraving
Company came in under separate favorable conditions.[2] Soon
after, in March 1859, Jones, Smillie and Edmonds were admitted as incorporators of the American Bank Note Company.

1) Altmann, op. cit., 7.

2) William H. Griffiths, The Story of the American
Bank Note Company (New York, 1959), 31.

Altmann assumed that they were awarded a substantial share
of the 4880 shares of unissued stock reserved for skillful
engraver employees.[3] Edmonds became a director in the
company in 1860 and the secretary the following year.
These offices were only terminated by his death.[4]

In both the Bank Note Engraving Company and the American Bank Note Company, Edmonds did not confine his activities to administration. A lengthy article on the American
Bank Note Company in Harper's, described their modeling and
designing rooms. "The walls are covered with original drawings by Darley, Casilear, Edmonds, Herrick and others.
Portfolios filled with such drawings are opened for our
inspection. A connoisseur in art could nowhere spend a
more pleasant day than here."[5] The New York Public Library
has a number of engravings from the Bank Note Engraving
Company that appear to be based on Edmonds' work from their
subject matter mentioned below.

The DAB named drawings that Edmonds made for notes,
among them "Sewing-Girl," "Grinding the Scythe," "Barn-
Yard" and "Mechanic."[6] Grinding the Scythe (Figure 20),
in oil, can be seen at the New-York Historical Society

---

3) Altmann, op. cit., 7.

4) Griffiths, op. cit., 87, 89.

5) Harper's New Monthly Magazine, XXIV (Feb. 1862),
308.

6) Holt, DAB, op. cit.

(Accession No. 1947.493). The painting is dated 1856, an
indication that the banknote drawing might have come afterwards. It might be considered a departure for Edmonds because the scene was placed out of doors, but it was not
because he, in essence, enclosed the space around his two
major figures. A virile young farmer is grinding the scythe
as a small negro boy, affectionately portrayed, turns the
whetstone. To one side and in the background, a wagon
drawn by oxen can be seen standing in a barn where its hay
is being unloaded. The geometrics and perspective are
accurate and the colors as good as usual. The strength
of the painting lies in the vigor of the figures and the
effectiveness of the composition. The topic may have been
suggested by Mount's picture of 1851, Who'll Turn the Grindstone (Figure 21), but Edmonds' version is entirely different.

Two pictures by Edmonds that were never exhibited were
in the A.M. Cozzens collection. They were the Old Man with
a Pipe and Sunday Evening Lecture. The Crayon in an article
on private collections said, "The principal figure in the
latter picture has rarely been excelled by the artist, for
character and successful rendering of humor."[7]

Edmonds exhibited two paintings at the NAD in 1856.
The Crayon carried a description of The Thirsty Drover, now
in the Atkins Museum of Fine Arts in Kansas City, Mo.,

7) Crayon, III (April 1856), 123.

prior to the show:

> ...a drover has stopped to obtain a drink
> from a country well, over it is one of the
> large sweeps to which a bucket is attached,
> a primitive machine common in our country-
> but which is fast disappearing before water
> rams and patent Egyptian bucket lifters of
> species of sakkashs. Near the well is a
> woman engaged in washing, and by her side
> two children, the house furnishes the back-
> ground on the left while on the right is a
> receding drove of cattle.[8]

All Talk and No Work (Figure 22) was criticized for

being less complete in its painting, telling no story and

lacking detail.[9] It is true that in comparison with other

Edmonds' works it lacks detail, but it adds a little land-

scape that can be seen through the window of the barn.

Inside a white farmhand and a black man stand talking. The

farmhand has stopped his work to talk and leans on his rake

as he faces the black man who is clad in tattered clothing

and old top hat. It is hard to know who is being criti-

cized the most. The painting is now held by the Brooklyn

Museum in Brooklyn, N.Y.

A letter from E.D. Nelson to A.B. Durand in 1856 gives

an unusual view of Edmonds at work in an unfamiliar situa-

tion. Nelson was reporting on a visit to Bronxville:

> I passed my time very pleasantly and I
> think profitably in Bronxville. Mr. Ed-
> monds and I attempted a road side study,
> sitting on the open way exposed to the view
> of all the passers by. He winced, and

---

8) Crayon, III (March 1856), 91.

9) Ibid., III (May 1856), 147.

> fidgeted considerably under the experience,
> but endured it better than I supposed he
> would. It was a novel study for me-the
> time being late afternoon with a glow of
> sun light showing through the trees and on
> the opposite bank which was finely colored
> and equally relieved by the green band of
> fallen earth...I feel that I learned some-
> thing and Edmonds is in good spirits and
> seems fairly imbued with the artistic ex-
> perience. You know how agreeable a man of
> his talents can make himself, and on the
> occasion he was overflowing with all that
> can make one like myself...happy...[10]

The above could be taken for evidence that Edmonds had

completely retired from business, but for the other data.

A letter dated April 29, 1856 to John Durand from Edmonds

said, "I was in N.Y. today & Monday and also on Saturday

but was so engaged on Harlem RR & with Mr. Kelly's funeral

that I got no time to go elsewhere."[11] Although Edmonds

must have been severely hurt by the Mechanics' Bank inci-

dent, he seemed to have recovered well. There is every in-

dication that he devoted more time to painting.

Time to Go Home was exhibited at the NAD in 1857 as

Time to Go. A description ran as follows: "...the parents

of a young girl hinting 'notice to quit' to her beau, by

raking out the fire, and getting ready to shut up for the

night, the clock-dial indicating the hour of ten-Time to

Go Home..."[12] The Crayon, in a typographical error attri-

buted the painting to J.W. Edmonds, but called it one of

10) Durand Papers, op. cit., E.D. Nelson to A.B.
Durand, Sept. 1, 1856.

11) Ibid., F.W. Edmonds to J. Durand.

12) Crayon, III (March 1856), 91.

his best works in years.[13]

The three pictures that Edmonds showed at the NAD in
1858 can be seen at the New-York Historical Society. They
are on permanent loan from the New York Public Library's
Stuart Collection. An 1858 review said, "Edmonds contri-
butes three works, The Pan of Milk (Figure 23), Bargaining
(Figure 24), and The Wind-Mill (Figure 25). The first has
a still-life in the foreground and in the background a child
carrying a pan of milk; the second, an old woman and a
country man bargaining for a turkey and the third a father
blowing upon a toy windmill, just made, for a wondering
child. The action and humor of the figures are as well expressed as any in his previous works."[14]

Bargaining is shown at the New-York Historical Society
under the incorrect title of The Christmas Turkey (Figure
24), number 50 in the Stuart Collection. This character
study appears to be another facet of Edmonds' mother, if
we follow our former line of reasoning. Two letters
written to John Durand in 1858 confirm the fact that all
three of the pictures from the NAD show that year were
sold to R.L. Stuart.

The first letter thanked Durand for being instrumental in the sale of two of his paintings from the

13) Crayon, IV (June 1857), 223.

14) Ibid., V (April 1858), 115.

exhibit.[15] The second letter clarified the matter. "I
do not like to lessen the value of my pictures by selling
them below my usual price, but as Mr. Stuart has purchased
the other two I would be willing to let him have the one
you refer to for $150. It is true that the picture is
painted on a smaller canvas than the "Wind Mill" but it
cost me quite as much time and labor."[16]

Edmonds' preoccupation with the price of his paintings
and his desire to maintain his prices was not unique to
him. Throughout the accounts of the AAU and the NAD, the
prices an artist could command were the standards of success.

The last painting that Edmonds ever exhibited at the
NAD was The New Bonnet in 1859. The Town and Country review said, "...one of Mr. Edmonds happiest efforts—the
story is well told, the characters sharply defined, with
a great deal of good detail...As a theme of humor and
universal sympathy it arrests attention and provokes mirth-
ful comment."[17] Another review added the information that
in it was a well-drawn humorous head of an old man.[18]

---

15) Durand Papers, op. cit., F.W. Edmonds to A.B.
Durand, April 14, 1858.

16) Ibid., April 18, 1858.

17) Town and Country, No. 25, n.v. (June 18, 1859), 2.

18) Crayon, VI (May 1859), 192.

When William Ranney died destitute in 1857, his col-
leagues held an auction of his sketches and some of their
own works; the proceeds of $5000 were presented to his
widow and children. Cummings, Durand and Edmonds acted
as trustees for the money and the event led to the foundation of the Artists' Fund Society of New York. They began
to present shows of their own in 1859 to raise funds.[19]

In 1858 a series of "Artists' Receptions" were begun
and set such a successful precedent that they were emulated
by Boston and Brooklyn, the latter with decided success.[20]
Edmonds showed a number of pictures at these shows. In
March 1858 he was represented by a sketch called First-
Step in Dancing and a still life.[21] The next month he
showed Reading the Scriptures (Figure 26) which was bought
by Cozzens according to Tuckerman.[22] This last painting
is in a private collection in New York. It exemplifies
Edmonds' painting technique and coloring. An old woman
sits by the cold fireplace on a sunny afternoon, reading
her Bible. Off to the side, the sunlight streams into a
tidy kitchen, that can be seen through the doorway. Both
rooms are filled with the little items of daily use and

---

19) Harris, op. cit., 263, 270.

20) Cummings, op. cit., 268-9.

21) Crayon, V (March 1858), 87.

22) Ibid., V (April 1858), 115; Tuckerman, Book of the
Artists, op. cit., Appendix.

there is a cloth in "Edmonds' red." The scene conveys a warm feeling of home, cleanliness and peace. A portrait of Lydia Worth Edmonds at the Columbia County Historical Society suggests that the woman in the painting may have been Edmonds' mother.

In March 1859, Edmonds' showed A Boy Playing a Flute to Two Intently Listening Negro Children at still another Artists' Reception.[23] A note in the weekly along with this item said, "As this is an experiment to dispose of first class works in our country by auction, we will reserve our comments farther than to say that the method, if properly conducted, seems admirable for artist and purchaser and worth consideration."[24]

In 1860 and thereafter, Edmonds did not exhibit at the NAD, but still acted on the Council and Arrangements Committee for 1860. There is evidence to support the notion that he was disenchanted with the NAD because of internal squabbles. Although the Annals carry no overt confirmation, it does ratify this opinion through the report of events. Two letters from the Durand papers tell of the storm beneath the surface. The first was from Edmonds to A.B. Durand and dealt with the problem of paying Mr. Niblo, owner of a property on 23rd Street and Fourth Avenue, in order to be freed of the obligation to build

23) Town and Country, n.v. (March 19, 1859), 2.

24) Ibid.

because of the war. Edmonds said, "We expect to be opposed
by Gen'l Cummings...we are as anxious as you are to be re-
lieved from this obligation to build; & now we have a
chance to get rid of it..."[25]

The matter was still hanging fire when John Durand
wrote to his father on Sept. 27, 1861:

> I have just seen Edmonds. He has "posted"
> me about Academy matters. I sum them up
> briefly. Mr. Mayes, Mr. Sturges' lawyer
> gave his opinion adverse to Cummings' which
> opinion Mr. C. still maintains and so
> peculiarly as to make both Edmonds and
> Sturges afraid of him. He will not consent
> to their and your wishes but talks in such
> a way as to make Edmonds and Sturges think
> it best not to fight him, but to manage him
> if they can as, in the first place to get
> the money now in trust subject to his order
> out of his hands; and in the next place to
> see enough Academicians privately and talk
> them over to some action that will prevail
> over Cummings without his knowing anything
> about it until the time to act at a meet-
> ing comes. Edmonds wants you to hold your-
> self in readiness to come down at any time
> in case matters approach such a shape as to
> enable the trustees to do anything them-
> selves. Sturges, Edmonds says, asked him
> if Cummings didn't drink and Edmonds asked
> me if I didn't think him crazy. What re-
> joices me is that they now see the intem-
> perate proceedings of the man whether sane
> mad or drunk.[26]

At the time these letters were being written, Durand
had already tendered his resignation to the NAD as president, for the same reasons that we assume Edmonds withdrew,

---

25) Durand Papers, op. cit., F.W. Edmonds to A.B.
Durand, Aug. 20, 1861.

26) Ibid., J. Durand to A.B. Durand, Sept. 27, 1861.

internal squabbling. In Cummings' account of the resignation, most naturally, he presents himself in an exemplary
light.[27] John Durand gives an entirely different story
that he supports with verbatim quotes from Daniel Huntington's Memorial Address for Asher B. Durand.[28] The stories
in the published works are totally contradictory, but the
unpublished letters support the theory that Cummings had
become so difficult to work with as to no longer make the
aggravation worthwhile. Furthermore, the release of the
trustees after the death of Edmonds and Leupp establishes
that the property was purchased from Niblo on Nov. 1,
1861, making it clear that Edmonds and Durand had lost
the battle with Cummings.[29]

   This would seem to be a valid explanation of why Edmonds had ceased exhibiting at the NAD, but did go on showing at the Artists' Fund Society. The painting that he
offered there in 1860 was called The Morning Lesson.[30]
The picture for 1861 was titled Out of Work and Nothing to
Do.[31] This is now titled Hard Times, present location unknown, and is signed and dated 1861 (Figure 27). This

---

27) Cummings, op. cit., 295-298.

28) Durand, op. cit., 182-3.

29) Durand Papers, op. cit., Release, Feb. 28, 1863.

30) Chronological Exhibition of the Brooklyn Art
Association Catalogue, April 1872.

31) Ibid.

picture shows that Edmonds had grown and developed as an artist. It includes some of his favorite devices, the still life in the foreground and the figure of a woman, seen through a doorway, in the background. The new dimension in his work appeared in his deft handling of the space and the flight of stairs that strengthened the entire composition. Although exhibited in 1861, it is suggested that the Panic of '57 provided the inspiration for the picture. A third picture was exhibited in 1862, but the catalogue listing is the only information available.[32]

The diary of 1854 implied that Edmonds painted portraits of friends and relatives as a matter of course and so this must be included in any estimate of his total production. Thus, the pictures that have been discussed in this essay represent about one third of those actually painted.

Edmonds died unexpectedly, Feb. 7, 1863, probably from heart failure. He had arisen early, presumably to visit the room of his children who were ill. He was found dead in an easy-chair near his own bed, by his wife who was alarmed at his prolonged absence.[33] The published funeral notices carried the information that special trains to Bronxville would be run by the Harlem railroad for those

---

32) Artists' Fund Society Catalogue 1862.

33) Cummings, op. cit., 319.

who wished to attend the ceremony on February 10th.[34]

Edmonds was aware in his lifetime that he drove himself too hard and even made certain resolutions which, if
carried out, would lead to "a good appetite, sleep soundly,
digest well and live happily and good health must follow
as a matter of course." He recognized that this might not
be easy to do and asked himself, "Can I do all this? my
reply shall be like the brave Miller's 'I WILL TRY.'"[35]
Let us measure his success.

The first requirement was that he restrain his ambition. He certainly failed in this because he achieved
enormous successes in his disparate fields. The Clearing
House stands today as testimony to his initiative and it
still uses a variation of the coin certificate he devised.
This achievement in banking was offset by his setback at
the Mechanics' Bank. Part of this must be laid to his inability to conform to his second requirement that he not be
anxious to do too much. The story of his frenetic accom-
plishments is overwhelming. It is doubtful that the next
several resolutions were complied with, "be patient; take
things easily; allow nothing to fret...submit to the changes
and chances of fortune with perfect good nature..." His
diary for '54 showed that the anxiety symptoms that followed
his breakdown persisted. The lengthy pamphlet that he

---

34) The New York Evening Post, Feb. 9, 1863.

35) Edmonds, "Travel Journal," op. cit., July 5,
1841.

published in his own defence after the embezzlement charge
in '55 established how very much he took these things to
heart.

His next two requirements met with more success.
"...Mingle freely with society; avoid being too much alone..."
Opportunities to be alone could not have been frequent.
After his second marriage, the children arrived rapidly and
the record of his business, social and artistic life shows
that there was little free time left. We cannot know
whether he read the travel books that was his next requirement, but we do know that he continued to read when he found
the time.

"...paint but little and rather for pleasure than
reputation..." This was a lost cause from the start, but
one that led to great success for him. In 1844, his autobiography recounted how he achieved his triumphs in painting, how original he had been when he painted the cool
greys in the fire in Sparking and of his membership in the
Sketch Club. All of the foregoing was boasting about his
triumphs. We don't know if he was able to, "...think slowly,
work slowly, eat slowly and walk slowly..." but we doubt
it very much.

At the very beginning of this essay we emphasized that
the most unusual facet of his life was his unique ability
to move freely across the lines of the artistic, cultural
and financial communities of New York and to mingle with

and influence its leaders. We think that this has been established beyond the prosaic words of the reference works
that have simply listed his memberships. His own modesty
plus the necessities of his business life did not always
permit him to take the limelight as he deserved. There is
sufficient evidence to show that his contributions were
substantial in every way and that circumstances and time
have reduced the acknowledgments due to him.

The charisma of his presence has been amply evoked by
the words of his friends, but their stalwart support of
him when he was in trouble showed that there was more to
him than that.

Edmonds' pictures have been dealt with at length, but
did he make a contribution to art as such? His sensitive
and sympathetic nature did result in vignettes of American life that might have had sentiment but never were
saccharine. His empathetic approach inferred that problems
could have humor and sadness combined. As one critic put
it, his pictures, "...are generally intended to make you
laugh, but often possess an undercurrent of philosophy,
which makes them voiceless preachers to the thoughtful
man."[36]

---

36) AAU Press Book, op. cit., Express, n.d.

APPENDIX

The Onderdonk Story

Benjamin Tredwell Onderdonk was ordained Bishop of
New York in 1830 to what was then the largest and most in-
fluential diocese in the country. By 1833 a High Church
movement began among American Episcopalians that advanced
pretty far and even led to some notable conversions to
Catholicism. When the American Protestant Episcopalian
Church was established in 1789, it began with three main
parties: the High Church with a prevailing Catholic tone;
the Broad Church that was hardly distinguishable from other
Protestant sects and the Evangelicals or Low Church whose
main significance was that they provided a succession of
recruits who otherwise might not have been led in that direc-
tion.

The leading ideas of the Oxford Movement, begun in
England in 1832, were published in New York in 1839 as the
Tracts for the Times. These were recommended to the students in the General Theological Seminary by Onderdonk who
was a member of the faculty. Onderdonk also publicly expressed some views favorable to the Tracts. By 1842, New
York became the center of American Tractarianism. One of
the most prominent students from this group, Arthur Carey,

came up for ordination and was refused on grounds of Roman
propensities by two men from the Evangelical group, Drs.
Hugh Smith and Henry Anthon. Carey was put on trial on
these charges. Everyone realized that it was not Carey
personally who was aimed at but rather the set he belonged
to and the faculty of the seminary.

Carey was acquitted by a verdict of six to two. The
two against were Smith and Anthon. Onderdonk reserved his
decision and did not cast a vote at all. While Carey's
ordination was in progress, the two accusers arose and in
formal language protested. Bishop Onderdonk replied that
Mr. Carey's orthodoxy had been enquired into and proved to
his satisfaction and then having characterized the inter-
ruption as 'scandalous' went on with the ordination.
Bishop Onderdonk, while not exactly a Tractarian, always
had protected students of the Carey type on the principle
that as Anglicans they had as much right to their views
as Evangelicals had to theirs.

The anti-Romanists were determined to have their way
and now they resorted to other methods. Charges of personal misconduct on the part of Onderdonk had been
whispered for some time and now these charges were pressed.
There were nine charges that under the influence of and
improperly excited by spiritous liquors the bishop had
manipulated his hands upon the persons of certain women
with impure intent. There was no suggestion that he proceeded any further. All the alleged offences dated between

1837 and 1841, a time before the canon under which the trial
was proceeded was adopted.

In view of the delicate character of some of the testimony, it is extraordinary that the court specifically
ordered the publication of the complete record of the
Proceedings, including the securing of the copyright. The
most serious of the allegations was completely disproved.
The opinion of one bishop was that Onderdonk was merely unfortunate in his manner, but this was the Victorian era
when the sexual taboo was at its height. The bishop's case
was not only sadly mishandled by himself and his advisors,
but in the fevered atmosphere, with all the publicity,
fair judgment was practically impossible.

On the other hand to believe that the Bishop was entirely innocent requires the alternative of "...four
females, young, sensitive, conscientous, and heretofore
of unsuspected truth and virtue, without concert and without motive, having each, year after year, and wholly unknown to each other deliberately concocted a story of
indecent and immoral conduct on the part of the Bishop..."

The Bishop was suspended and this was to be his
sentence, for it was never removed. The greatest fault
shown by the Bishop in the matter, according to his friends,
was indiscretion, but he was tried, convicted and sentenced,
not for indiscretion or imprudence, but for immorality
with a deliberately impure intent.

Knowing he was dying, Onderdonk declared his innocence, stating that his conscience acquitted him in the sight of God. His funeral was held on May 7, 1861 and the <u>New York Express</u> of May 8 gave this account of the funeral: "Few more suggestive spectacles have ever been witnessed in New York...The immense concourse...crowded to pay respect to his memory..."

Bibliography

<u>An Appeal and Review from the Sentence of the Bishop of New York and A Review of the Trial</u> (New York, 1845). From the Buffalo Commercial Advertiser.

Chadwick, Owen. <u>The Mind of the Oxford Movement</u> (Stanford, 1960).

Chorley, E. Clowes. "Benjamin Tredwell Onderdonk, Fourth Bishop of New York," <u>Historical Mag. of the Protestant Episcopal Church</u>, Vol. IX (Mar. 1940), pp. 2-44.

DeMille, George E., M.A. <u>The Catholic Movement in the American Episcopal Church</u> (Phila., 1950).

King, Charles, ed. of New-York American. <u>A Review of the Trial of the Rt. Rev. B.T. Onderdonk, D.D.</u> (New York, 1845).

Ryan, Edwin. "The Oxford Movement in the United States," <u>Catholic Historical Review</u>, Vol. XIX (April 1933), pp. 33-49.

BIBLIOGRAPHY

Primary Documents

Altmann, Sol. E.P.S. No. 25. United States Designers and
Engravers of Bank Notes and Stamps (New York Public
Library, Print Room, Unpublished Mss., 1961).

Bryant, William Cullen. Papers (New York Public Library,
Mss. Division).

Coffey, Father William Samuel. Commemorative Discourse,
Oct. 24, 1865 (St. Paul's Episcopal Church, Eastchester, N.Y.).

Coffey, Father William Samuel. Notes (St. Paul's Episcopal Church, Eastchester, N.Y.).

Durand, Asher B. and Durand, John. Papers (New York Public
Library, Mss. Division).

Edmonds, Francis William. Autobiography, I, II, III
(Francis Edmonds Tyng, New Jersey).

Edmonds, Francis William. Diary 1854 (Author).

Edmonds, Francis William. Folder (New York Public Library,
Art Division).

Edmonds, Francis William. Travel Journal (2 vols., Columbia
County Historical Society, Kinderhook, N.Y.).

Flagg, Azariah Cutting. Papers (New York Public Library,
Mss. Division).

Kensett, John Frederick. Diary (Frick Art Reference
Library, June 1, 1840-May 31, 1841).

Kensett, John Frederick. Papers (New York State Library,
Albany, History and Archives).

New York City Archives. "Death certificate of Francis N.
Edmonds" (Jan. 5, 1840), /Martha N. Edmonds/.

Records. (St. Paul's Episcopal Church, Eastchester, N.Y.).

Personal Interviews and Correspondence

Frankenstein, Alfred. Lectures (Metropolitan Museum of Art, June-July 1970).

Janson, Horst, W. (November 11, 1971).

Novak, Barbara. (May 1969).

West, Canon Edward N., Th. D., sub-dean of the Cathedral of St. John the Divine (May 21, 1971).

Wetzel, Mrs. Ethel., Personal Secretary to Mrs. Dwight D. Eisenhower, Correspondence with Maybelle Mann in 1970.

Published Primary Documents

Dunlap, William. Diary of William Dunlap (3 vols., New York, 1930).

Edmonds, Francis William. Defence of Francis W. Edmonds, Late Cashier of the Mechanics' Bank, Against the Charges Preferred Against Him by Its President and Cashier (New York, 1855).

Knapp, Shepherd. Letter to the Stockholders of the Mechanics' Bank in Reply to the Defence of Francis W. Edmonds, Their Late Cashier (New York, 1855).

Nevins, Allan and Halsey, Milton Thomas, editor. The Diary of George Templeton Strong, Young Man in New York, 1835-1849 (New York, 1952).

Secondary Works

Andrews, Wayne. Architecture, Ambition and Americans (New York, 1967).

Baker, Paul R. The Fortunate Pilgrims (Cambridge, Mass., 1964).

Brock, Lucien. The Bench and Bar of New York (2 vols., New York, 1870).

Burnet, John. A Treatise on Painting in Four Parts (London, 1850).

Callow, James T. Kindred Spirits (Chapel Hill, 1967).

Chadwick, Owen. The Mind of the Oxford Movement (Stanford, 1960).

Cooper, James Fenimore. The Spy (New York, 1946).

Cowdrey, Mary Bartlett. American Academy of Fine Arts and American Art-Union, Introduction and Exhibition Record 1816-1852 (2 vols., New York, 1953).

Cowdrey, Mary Bartlett. National Academy of Design and Its Catalogues to 1860 and National Academy of Design Exhibition Record 1826-1860 (2 vols., New York, 1943).

Cummings, Thomas Seir. Historic Annals of the National Academy of Design (Philadelphia, 1865).

Cunningham, Allan. The Life of Sir David Wilkie (3 vols., London, 1843).

Cunningham, Allan. The Lives of the Most Eminent British Painters and Sculptors (3 vols., New York, 1835).

Cunningham, Allan. The Lives of the Most Eminent British Painters and Sculptors (6 vols., New York, 1832).

DeMille, George E. The Catholic Movement in the Episcopal Church (Philadelphia, 1950).

Dickens, Charles. The Posthumous Papers of the Pickwick Club (London, n.d.).

Dummelow, Rev. J.R., ed. Commentary on the Holy Bible by Various Writers (New York, 1958).

Dunlap, William. History of the Rise and Progress of the Arts of Design in the United States (2 vols., New York, 1969).

Durand, John. The Life and Times of A.B. Durand (New York, 1894).

Flexner, James T. That Wilder Image (New York, 1962).

Graves, Algernon, F.S.A. Royal Academy of Arts (8 vols., London, 1905).

Griffiths, William H. The Story of the American Bank Note Company (New York, 1959).

Groce, George C. and Wallace, David H. The New-York Historical Society's Dictionary of Artists in America 1564-1860 (New Haven, Fourth Printing, Sept. 1969).

Hamilton, Sinclair. Early American Book Illustrators and Wood Engravers, 1670-1870 (Princeton, 1958).

Hammond, Bray. Banks and Politics in America (Princeton, 1857).

Harris, Neil. The Artist in American Society. The Formative Years 1790-1860 (New York, 1961).

Hawthorne, Nathaniel. The Marble Faun (New York, 1961).

Irving, Washington. The Sketch Book of Geoffrey Crayon, Gent. (New York, n.d.).

King, Charles, editor of the New-York American. A Review of the Trial of the Rt. Rev. B.T. Onderdonk, D.D. (New York, 1845).

Larkin, Oliver W. Art and Life in America (Revised ed., New York, 1966).

Morris, Richard B., ed. Encyclopedia of American History (New York, 1961).

Putnam, George. American Facts (London, 1845).

Raymond, William. Biographical Sketches of the Distinguished Men of Columbia County (Albany, 1851).

Redlich, Fritz. History of American Business Leaders, Part I-Men and Ideas 1781-1840; Part II-The Molding of American Banking, Men and Ideas 1840-1910 (New York, 1951).

Richardson, E.P. Painting in America (New York, 1965).

Rutledge, Anna Wells. Pennsylvania Academy Cumulative Record of Exhibition Catalogues (Philadelphia, 1955).

Sandby, William. The History of the Royal Academy of Arts (2 vols., London, 1862).

Schlesinger, Jr. Arthur. The Age of Jackson (New York, 1946).

Shoemaker, Samuel M. Calvary Church Yesterday and Today, A Centennial History (New York, 1936).

Smollett, Tobias. Peregrine Pickle (New York, 1964).

Taylor, George Rogers. The Transportation Revolution 1815-1860 (New York, 1951).

Thornbury, Walter. British Artists from Hogarth to Turner (2 vols., London, 1861).

Tuckerman, Henry T. Artist's Life; or Sketches of American Painters (New York, 1847).

Tuckerman, Henry T. Book of the Artists (2 vols., New York, 1867).

Tunnard, Christopher and Reed, Henry Hope. American Skyline (New York, 1956).

Tyler, Alice Felt. Freedom's Ferment (New York, 1962).

Vail, R.W.G. Knickerbocker Birthday (New York, 1954).

Weitenkampf, Frank. American Graphic Art (Revised ed., New York, 1924).

Whitley, William T. Art in England 1800-1837 (2 vols., Cambridge, 1930).

Catalogues

Artists' Fund Society (1859-1862).

Chronological Exhibition of the Brooklyn Art Association (April 1872).

Mount, William Sidney, Alfred Frankenstein (Washington, 1968).

Musee Royal, Explication des Ouvrages de Peinture, Sculpture, Architecture, Gravure et Lithographie (Paris, 1841).

National Academy of Design (1829-1854).

New York Gallery of Fine Arts (1848).

Parke-Bernet (Jan. 6-8, 1949).

Articles

Benizet, E. "T. Saulini," Dictionnaire des Peintres, Sculpteurs, Dessinateurs et Graveurs (11 vols., France 1954), VII, 534.

Brush, Sybil. "The Story Begins with an Artist," The Villager (Bronxville, N.Y., March 1966, n.v.).

Chorley, C. Clowes. "Benjamin Tredwell Onderdonk, Fourth Bishop of New York," Historical Magazine of the Protestant Episcopal Church, IX (March 1940), 1-51.

Holt, Jean MacKinnon. "Francis William Edmonds," in Allen Johnson ed., Dictionary of American Biography (11 vols., New York, 1927-58), III, 22.

Lesley, Parker E. "Thomas Cole and the Romantic Sensibility," Art Quarterly, III (Fall 1942).

Ryan, Edwin. "The Oxford Movement in the United States," Catholic Historical Review, XIX (April 1933), 33-49.

Unsigned Articles

American Art-Union Bulletin (April 1849---December 1851).

Broadway Journal (April 1845---July 1845).

The Crayon (1855-61).

Harper's New Monthly Magazine, XXIV (Feb. 1862).

The Knickerbocker (1836-1863).

Literary World (April 1847---December 1853).

New York Mirror (1829-1846).

Town and Country (1846-1863).

Newspapers

American Art-Union Press Book, Newspaper Clippings (1847-1852).

Commercial Advertiser, May 11, 1838---April 27, 1846.

New York Evening Post, Jan. 20 and 27, 1843.

New York Times, Sept. 30, 1854.

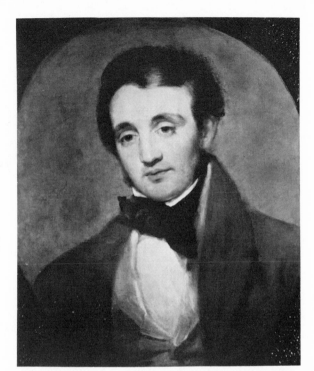

Figure 1.

Francis
William
Edmonds:
Self-portrait,
oil on canvas.

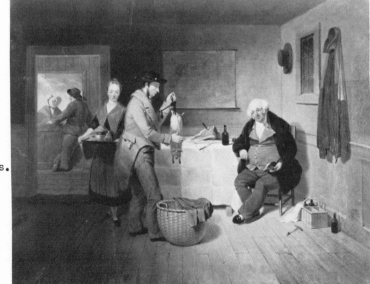

Figure 2.

Francis
William
Edmonds:
The Epicure,
oil on canvas.

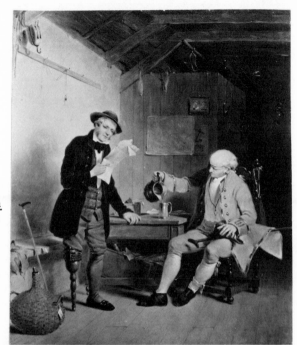

Figure 3.

Francis
William
Edmonds:
Commodore Trunnion
and Jack Hatchway,
oil on canvas.

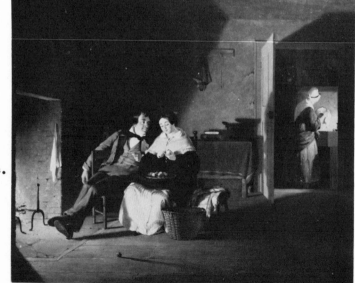

Figure 4.

Francis
William
Edmonds:
Sparking,
oil on canvas.

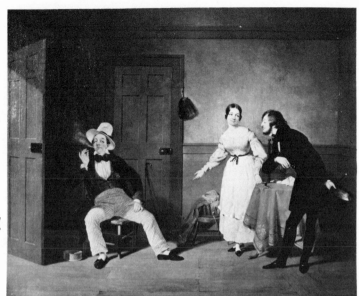

Figure 5.

Francis
William
Edmonds:
The City and
Country Beaux,
oil on canvas.

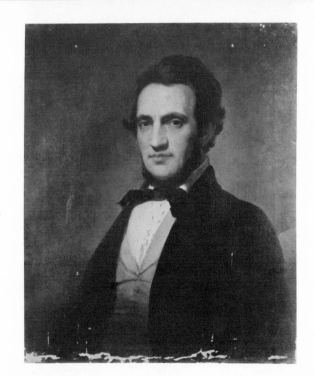

Figure 6.

Asher B. Durand:
Portrait of Francis
William Edmonds,
oil on canvas.

Figure 7.

Francis
William
Edmonds:
The Image
Peddler, oil
on canvas.

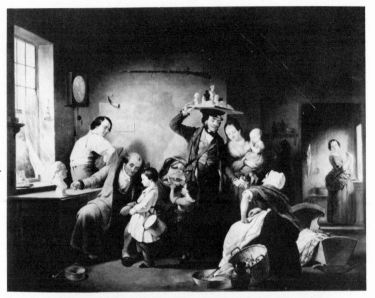

Figure 8.

Francis
William
Edmonds:
Head of a man,
oil on canvas.

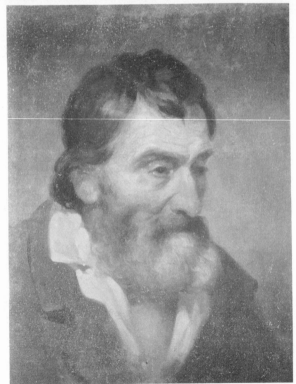

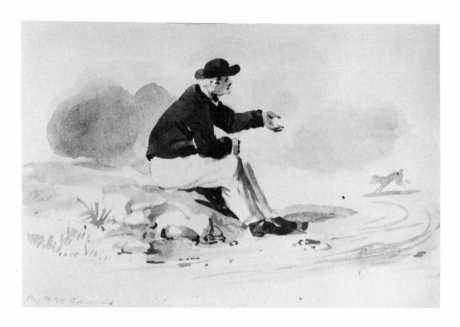

Figure 9. Francis William Edmonds: sketch,
pencil and wash.

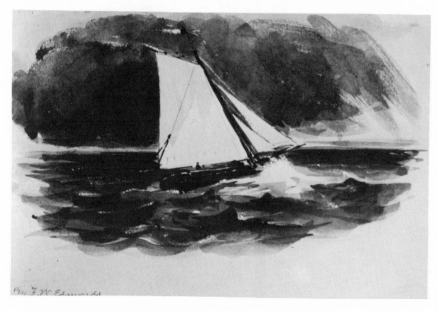

Figure 10. Francis William Edmonds: sketch,
pencil and wash.

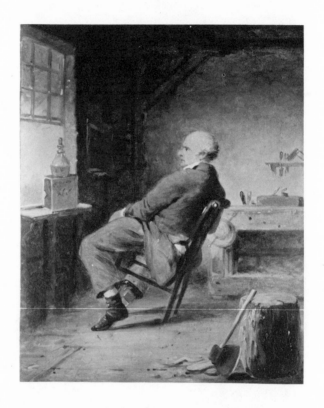

Figure 11. Francis William Edmonds:
Facing the Enemy,
oil on board.

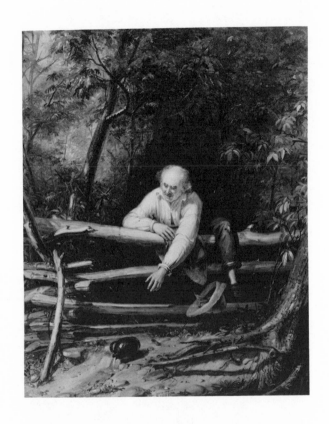

Figure 12. William Sidney Mount:
Loss and Gain
oil on canvas.

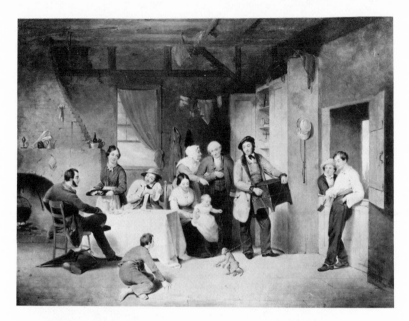

Figure 13.   Francis William Edmonds: The Organ-Grinder,
oil on canvas. Exhibited as The Strolling
Musician, 1848.

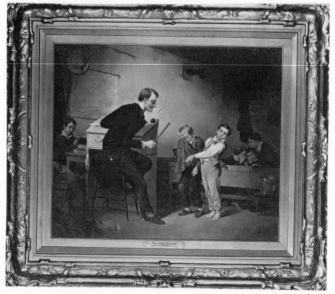

Figure 14.   Francis William Edmonds: The Schoolmaster,
oil on canvas. Exhibited as The Two Culprits,
1850.

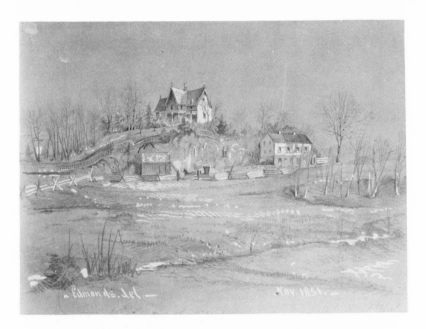

Figure 15. Francis William Edmonds: Crow's Nest, gouache on brown paper.

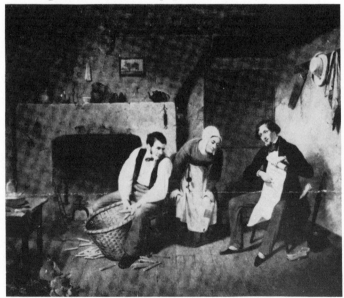

Figure 16. Francis William Edmonds: The Real Estate Agent, oil on canvas. Exhibited as The Speculator, 1852.

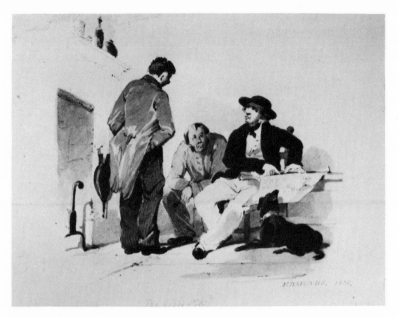

Figure 17.   Francis William Edmonds: The Paper City,
wash drawing.

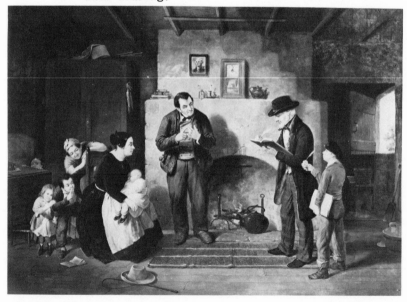

Figure 18.   Francis William Edmonds: Taking the Census,
oil on canvas.

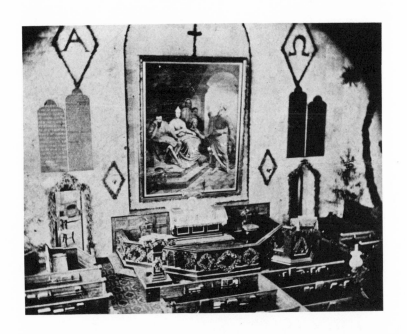

Figure 19.   Francis William Edmonds: Felix Trembled, oil
on canvas, as seen in St. Paul's Episcopal Church,
Eastchester, N.Y.

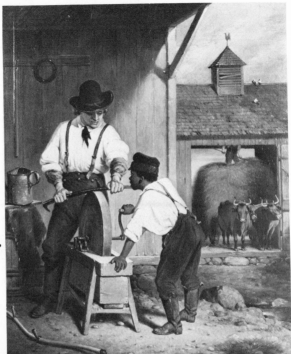

Figure 20.

Francis William Edmonds: The Scythe Grinder oil on canvas.

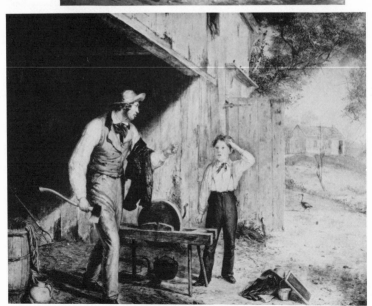

Figure 21. William Sidney Mount: Who'll Turn the Grindstone, oil on canvas.

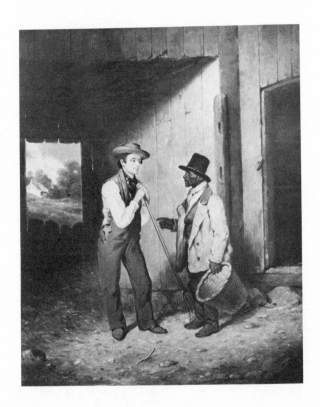

Figure 22.   Francis William Edmonds: <u>All Talk and No Work</u>,
oil on canvas.

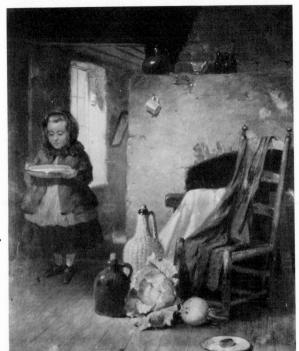

Figure 23.

Francis
William
Edmonds:
The Pan
of Milk
oil on canvas.

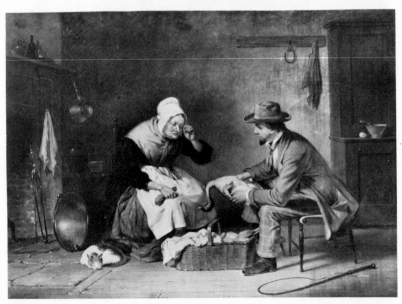

Figure 24. Francis William Edmonds: The Christmas Turkey,
            oil on canvas. Exhibited as Bargaining, 1858.

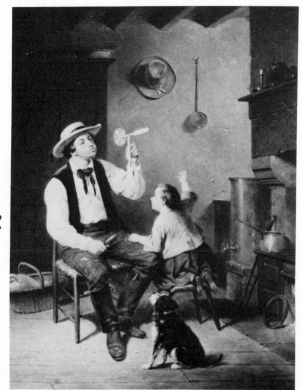

Figure 25.

Francis
William
Edmonds:
The Wind-Mill,
oil on canvas.

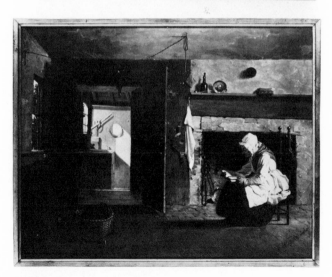

Figure 26.   Francis William Edmonds: Reading the
Scriptures, oil on canvas.

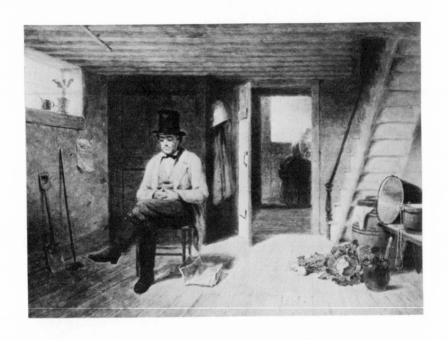

Figure 27. Francis William Edmonds: Hard Times, oil
on canvas. Exhibited as Out of Work and
Nothing to Do, 1861.